D0014802

It's Not as Bad as You Think

Why Capitalism Trumps Fear and the Economy Will Thrive

Brian S. Wesbury

John Wiley & Sons, Inc.

Published by John Wiley & Sons, Inc., Hoboken, New Jersey.
Published simultaneously in Canada.

For general information on our other products and services or for technical support, please contact our Customer Care Department within the United States at (800) 762-2974, outside the United States at (317) 572-3993 or fax (317) 572-4002.

Wiley also publishes its books in a variety of electronic formats. Some content that appears in print may not be available in electronic books. For more information about Wiley products, visit our web site at www.wiley.com.

Library of Congress Cataloging-in-Publication Data

Wesbury, Brian S.
It's not as bad as you think : why capitalism trumps fear and the economy will thrive / Brian S. Wesbury.
p. cm.
Includes bibliographical references and index.
ISBN 978-0-470-23833-2 (cloth)
1. Capitalism. 2. Economic forecasting. 3. Global Financial Crisis, 2008-2009. I. Title.
HB501.W4855 2010
330.12'2—dc22

2009035137

Printed in the United States of America
10 9 8 7 6 5 4 3 2

To Kyle and Graham
My fervent prayer is that both of you live in a time and place that allows your God-given talents to be multiplied in a way that improves the lives of all people.

Thank you both for your love and understanding.
You mean more to me than words will ever express.

. . . children are a heritage from the Lord . . .
Psalm 127:3

Contents

Foreword

This is an important book. That's because optimism really is critical to recovery. An optimistic country is a country that can find its way to growth. What the author, Brian Wesbury, suggests, however, is that the quality of that growth depends on the kind of optimism at issue. An optimism of shopping alone does not move the United States forward—especially when that spending and shopping is directed by the government. Rather, it is an optimism of innovation or spirit that moves America forward—and that kind of optimism comes, mostly, from outside government. Such optimism emanates from the private sector, but also from what one might call the spiritual sector—that area of our lives that is mostly profoundly individual.

Our government knows the power that businesses and individuals can have and tends to be envious of it. Therefore, even as it calls for hope, Washington will sometimes try to obscure the prospect of plenty that a business, an industry, or an individual, represents. Washington will also argue that private-sector growth is problematic, and that only a government brand of growth is good. It's a weird line to take, but governments do take it. To what extent, however, comes clear only with a review of past downturns and recoveries.

Consider, to start with, the period of the Great Depression. The standard narrative has it that President Franklin Roosevelt shone a light of optimism in a dark time. On a personal level, that is true. Roosevelt, through his radio addresses, inspired citizens. The line Americans recall is "the only thing we have to fear is fear itself."

We also learned in school that Roosevelt's policies were premised on optimism and the possibility of growth. Upon examination, however, this second argument does not hold up. In 1932, before he became president, Roosevelt gave a grim speech at the Commonwealth Club of San Francisco. There, Governor Roosevelt recalled the analysis of the scholar Frederick Jackson Turner that with the close of America's geographic frontier would come also the end of the age of plenty. Growth prospects in the private sector just weren't the same as they had once been, FDR said, and the days of blithe hope were over: "Equality of opportunity as we have known it no longer exists. Our industrial plant is built; the problem just now is whether under existing conditions it is overbuilt." In a new and smaller America, the best plan was to allow government to redistribute. America's task now, said Roosevelt, was "the soberer, less dramatic business of administering resources and plants already in hand, of seeking to reestablish foreign markets for our surplus production, of meeting the problem of underconsumption, of adjusting production to consumption, of distributing wealth and products more equitably, of adapting existing economic organizations to the service of the people."

Today, we know the presumption that the United States could not grow beyond the levels of 1929 was absurd. The geographic frontier gave rise to the industrial frontier, which gave rise to the information frontier. But that presumption of decline did inform the New Deal, and did hurt the U.S. economy. The New Dealers repeatedly raised taxes, in part to get revenue to subsidize their redistribution, but also on the premise that businesses' well-being was not especially important to the future. Indeed, FDR blamed hopeful capitalists as "princes of property" who prevented growth.

Less known than the tax legislation, but probably more important, was the New Deal policy on utilities. In every business cycle, there is one industry so exciting that it is almost recession-proof. In the 1930s, that industry was utilities. Half of the country was wired, but half was not—the South. "The South is tired of living in the dark," as the line ran. Both Southerners and Northerners understood the productivity gains that wiring the nation would deliver. Wall Street also understood, and spent considerable energy cobbling together companies large enough for multistate ventures. The industry leaders knew that utilities had enormous power to grow if only they could marshal the capital for their projects.

A logical Washington would have let utilities "plentify" so they might help pull the nation out of the slump. Instead, however, the New Dealers saw the utilities as a threat to their own hope monopoly. The New Dealers therefore vilified private companies and private utility lines laid by companies such as Commonwealth and Southern as "spite lines." They persecuted the private companies in the courts. And lawmakers on Capitol Hill passed a law that slew the utilities industry—the so-called "death sentence" act that restricted the industry's crucial ability to marshal capital. Government utilities, by contrast, were subsidized and supported, the Tennessee Valley Authority being the grand example. But time proved that the TVA and institutions like it could not pull the country out of depression.

The idea that government was the only source of plenty even extended into the area of religion. It is no accident that some of Roosevelt's greatest enemies were church leaders or community leaders. They understood that the New Deal through its expansion was effectively demanding that the church and the charitable movement retreat. Scholar David Beito has shown that the federal government's expansion did indeed squeeze private charity and fraternal societies out of the business of caring for our country's needy.

The Great Society of Lyndon Johnson demonstrated a similar dynamic. President Johnson's plan seemed to be all about hope—the hope that a rich America could afford a larger government making generous outlays so that poorer Americans might finally enjoy a higher standard of living. Johnson was a big man physically, and his projects seemed both big and hopeful. Richard Nixon, Johnson's successor, likewise talked about hope.

As the Great Society unfolded, however, a new smallness began arriving on the scene. The leaders were telling the country, in essence, that the market could not take care of the rest. Politicians in the 1960s and 1970s were not content to confine their ambition to the United States. Through institutions like the World Bank they also preached their message of scarcity worldwide.

The most famous example of this attitude was the Club of Rome, an international group of experts who believed that private sector growth itself was problematic. The *New York Times* headline for one of their meetings was "Warning on Growth Perils Is Examined at Symposium." The Indian ambassador at the meeting delivered a line that was typical for the time: "No growth would have to reflect a more equal state of affairs"; less growth was better because it yielded greater equality. This was a period when most of the world believed places like India and China could not match population growth with economic growth.

No one personified the arrogance of this attitude better than Robert McNamara during his period as head of the World Bank. In 1969 McNamara sought a venue to deliver his message of population control. He chose Notre Dame University. This was his way of saying that any nongovernment hope—private-sector hope, religious hope—was not as important as restraining human reproduction. The possibility that he could be wrong about population growth did not occur to McNamara.

The fact that in the interim India and China have demonstrated they can grow seems to have had little effect on arguments or political leaders. Today, our government likewise senses a threat from the private sector, and likewise envies activity that is not part of government. From Washington to our towns you hear the argument that public intervention is needed in health care because health care is in trouble.

But there's another explanation: Health care is a hopeful industry with great potential for economic growth. Now that they can prolong their lives, people often will spend to do so. Government wants to capture control of this growth industry. To make the argument for their own importance to optimism and growth, our government and others are willing to impose a culture of scarcity. In this period, it is not zero population growth that is the goal but rather new green regulations. We think of Washington's policy of a green recovery as a good thing. But, in fact, a green recovery is a slower recovery that advantages Washington in its competition with the private sector.

The only check on this dynamic is the private sector itself. It has the capacity to outgrow government. Over time, individuals and their businesses will demonstrate that plenty is still possible for the United States. Brian Wesbury, of all thinkers, understands this best. Plenty is the goal, and this book is the primer on how to get there.

—Amity Shlaes

Amity Shlaes is senior fellow in economic history at the Council on Foreign Relations and author of a forthcoming biography of Calvin Coolidge.

Introduction

Next to the second coming of Christ and the Chicago Cubs winning the World Series, the end of capitalism may be the most predicted and expected event of humankind. In fact, many believe that we are locked in war between economic heaven and hell right now. And at the beginning of 2009, most would have been hard pressed to believe that hell hadn't won.

Rarely had the business of doom and gloom sold so well. The bookstores were filled with pessimism. Here are the titles of just some of the books published in the past year or so—*The Return of Depression Economics*;[1] *The Great Depression Ahead*;[2] *The Greatest Depression of All Time*;[3] *America's Financial Apocalypse*;[4] *Crash Proof: How to Profit from the Coming Economic Collapse*;[5] and *Financial Armageddon*.[6]

Outside of Alan Greenspan and a few who work for President Obama, the most famous economist alive was New York University Professor Nouriel Roubini, otherwise known as Dr. Doom. He was everywhere during the downturn. And his interviews on television and in newspapers and magazines were filled with forecasts of deep recession, skyrocketing unemployment, and deeper financial crisis.

There is no doubt that the economy suffered great pain. Housing prices were falling sharply, the stock market fell by more than 50 percent, the unemployment rate rose to its highest level in over 25 years. Some of the nation's biggest banks and investment banks failed, housing foreclosures grew rapidly, real gross domestic product (GDP) fell sharply, and the government intervened in the private sector to a greater extent than it had since the Great Depression.

None of us has ever seen anything like it. The question is: What in the world happened? Did the capitalist system finally fail? Did greed run rampant? Was government asleep at the switch? Was the financial crisis, as President Obama said, caused by "a perfect storm of irresponsibility"?[7]

But just as these questions were being wrestled with, the markets turned upward. As this book goes to press, major global stock indices, including those in the United States, have rallied by 50 percent or more over the previous six-month period. Economic data began to improve; even housing showed signs of a strong recovery. Fear of Great Depression II began to wane.

This recovery in the markets and economy created a whole new set of questions. Was it government stimulus that turned the economy around? Was the recovery fragile and in need of even more stimulus to make sure it didn't fall again? Was the economy in for a long period of underperformance, a "new normal" that would be bland and slow? Did the United States need to rebuild its economy in a different way to keep this from happening again?

Conventional wisdom answered all of these questions with a narrative that presupposes the failure of capitalism. The story goes something like this. Things were good for a long time, so investors and consumers alike began to make decisions that put them at risk. They borrowed too much, leveraged too much, and took too much risk. When small things started to go wrong, the interconnected nature of the financial system began to crack. And because the system had pushed itself beyond the point of no return and was under so much pressure, once that first crack appeared, it shattered like a piece of fine crystal.

This narrative benefits those who do not believe in capitalism. This narrative supports massive interference in the economy by the government. It is straight from the mind of John Maynard Keynes, who became famous in the 1930s for suggesting that people were driven by "animal spirits" and government must intervene to correct and fix their mistakes. In order to jump-start the economy when consumers emotionally pulled back, government must spend to provide a jolt to the economy.

In 1971, Richard Nixon is credited with saying, "We are all Keynesians now." That statement represented status quo thinking in the 1970s. But, looking back over the past two years, it is even more characteristic of the conventional wisdom today. President Bush pushed for the first stimulus plan in February 2008 and got a bipartisan $168 billion tax rebate bill through Congress. Moreover, an alphabet soup of Treasury Department and Federal Reserve special purpose investment vehicles were begun in 2008 and have already spent trillions.

While Republicans did not support the second stimulus—a $787 billion package of small tax cuts and big spending initiatives passed by Democrats in February 2009—their support for stimulus and government interference in 2008 had already set the stage. Once you have voted for stimulus or lobbied in favor of government interference, arguing against more seems hypocritical. Not since the 1970s have political leaders and influential editorial pages, on both sides of the aisle, supported such massive government programs.

The question is: Why? After watching how easy money, big-government spending, high tax rates, the redistribution of income, and regulation destroyed things in the 1970s, creating a stagflation that sent the economy into a tailspin, why would we ever go back? And European countries, with bigger governments than the United States, have much higher unemployment rates. Why would the United States want to emulate those policies? With Keynesian ideas seemingly refuted, why did they make such a comeback?

These are the questions this book wrestles with. The conclusions are decidedly different than the conventional wisdom. This was a crisis that never had to happen. But once it gathered momentum, it carried just about everyone, even normally stalwart supporters of free markets, right along with it. People panicked. Maybe all these years of success have made us soft. Maybe our psyche has become so fragile that we allow a small problem to be blown up in our minds into a huge problem. Like fearing the bogeyman under the stairs, we became terrified of something that just wasn't there.

My analysis of the economic causes and consequences of our recent economic panic leads me to believe that the economy is nowhere near as bad as many people make it out to be. The title of this book, *It's Not as Bad as You Think*, is a direct response to the unbelievable and unwarranted onslaught of negativity this country has been subjected to in the past few years.

Those who are strong enough to avoid behaving like lemmings, buying into the Armageddon story line, have the opportunity to profit handsomely. Listening to the dour prognostications of the conventional wisdom, and staying out of stocks, has already cost many worried investors nearly 50 percent. Unfortunately, many market participants did miss because they bought into the pessimism.

History shows that following the bears is a recipe for mediocrity or worse. They may be right over short periods of time, but they have always failed over the longer term. Ironically, however, if politicians and voters behave as if the conventional wisdom is correct, and the economy needs more government and less capitalism, we will head down the wrong path, making it even more difficult to create wealth in the future.

It's important for you to know that I rarely subscribe to what most people call conventional wisdom. Almost three decades of experience as a business economist has taught me that the most popular story line—the favorite explanation for whatever is going on—is probably wrong. This does not mean I am a contrarian. I am a supply-sider. And in a world that follows the teachings of John Maynard Keynes, a supply-sider is by definition in the minority.

This book is my interpretation, a supply-side interpretation, of the world as it stands today, and what the future has in store for those willing to look beyond the conventional wisdom.

Dealing with Criticism

Because economics has become so political, my stance on the economy has made me something of a lightning rod. Some of these attacks are ad hominem and are not worthy of a second thought, but there are two criticisms that deserve response.

The first criticism is that I am a perma-bull—someone who is always optimistic about the economy. This is not true. In 2000, at the peak of dot-com bull market, I was one of only six (out of 54) economists in the *Wall Street Journal*'s forecasting poll who predicted a recession for 2001. The recession happened and I ended up the number one forecaster in 2001.

Finishing number one in this survey takes a great deal of luck, so I do not say this to brag about my performance. Any of the six of us that forecast recession could have finished number one, but it just so happened that my numbers were a little closer. It's not the number one finish that matters all that much, but the fact that I went on record predicting a recession. This is something a perma-bull would never do.

Second, there are many who note that I missed the recession of 2008. This is true. Right up through mid-September 2008, I believed that the economy could absorb subprime loan losses without experiencing a true recession. But once Lehman Brothers was allowed to fail, Hank Paulson proposed the $700 billion Troubled Asset Repurchase Plan (TARP), and President Bush gave a primetime speech that scared people half to death, an economic panic began.

For the record, I was not in denial about the extent of damage in the housing market. Clearly, housing was in free fall, which was causing a loss of jobs (in construction), slower industrial production (of housing-related materials), and other damage to the economy. But GDP—excluding housing—was still rising. The nonhousing economy, which represented roughly 96 percent of all economic activity, was still growing right up through July or August 2008.

What caused the crisis to spread and turn into a full-blown panic was mark-to-market accounting. During the first half of 2008, I continued to believe that the government would lean on the Financial Accounting Standards Board (FASB) to reform mark-to-market accounting rules. But it didn't. In fact, the Paulson Treasury Department used mark-to-market rules to put pressure on banks and financial institutions. This was a huge mistake. It turned a significant problem into a catastrophe. And then, as these accounting rules deepened the crisis, the government interfered in the private sector more and more.

I will go to my grave believing that if the government had just done the right thing—suspend mark-to-market accounting and avoid interfering in the system—the United States could have avoided a recession in 2008. But because the government did not do this, and decided that it must interfere in the financial system, the recession became inevitable. The economy went into free fall. This was the first true panic the United States has experienced since the Panic of 1907.

Having Faith

But if you know anything about American economic history, you know that the Panic of 1907 ended after about a year, and the stock market and economy returned to strong growth. After falling 49 percent in 1907, the Dow Jones Industrial Average increased more than 60 percent during its recovery in 1908. And don't forget, the Chicago Cubs won the World Series in 1908 as well. As a Cubs fan and a supply-side optimist, I suspect that the next few years could be very good years indeed.

In 1907 and 1908 there was no income tax, the federal government was very small, and federal regulation was virtually nonexistent. In other words, the economy did not need government to recover because capitalism is robust and resilient, not brittle and unbalanced. It was experiences like this, the consistent progress of the economy and improvement in living standards, that helped define the uniquely

American optimism that so many observers have recognized throughout history. This optimism can alternatively be described as a faith that things would keep getting better.

But for some reason, many Americans now seem to have developed a strange kind of fatalism to go along with their faith. It's almost as if success has bred a new kind of fear. The higher we climb, the greater the fear that we will fall. Part of this fear comes from government itself. Politicians want to be seen as saviors, so they don't mind having fear in the air. It creates demand for their services.

Keynesian theory fans these flames of doubt—it says capitalism is unstable and government has the ability to correct that. But Keynesian economic theory has been proven wrong time after time. There is nothing wrong with capitalism; it is not broken. Losing faith would be a mistake. In the end, that is the message of this book.

And that's the good news here. For more than 200 years, American capitalism has proven its resilience. It has persevered. And it will do so again as long as fear and fatalism do not prove to be its undoing. My fervent belief is that, once again, as it has so many times in history, America will climb from the ashes of the current crisis and move forward as an economic leader. Specifically, I think in the next 12 to 18 months an economic boom will lift stocks and economic activity sharply.

This does not mean that the United States can't or won't head back into the wilderness of big-government spending and high tax rates in the years ahead. It may. As a result, investors need two sets of strategies. One to take advantage of the current boom and one to stay alive if the leader of global capitalism heads into the wilderness. These questions and these strategies are what this book deals with. Thanks for picking it up—I hope it helps build your faith in the amazing benefits of free market capitalism.

Chapter 1

Getting the Right Perspective

Many people are calling the recession and financial crisis of 2007–2009—what this book will call the Panic of 2008—the worst economic calamity since the Great Depression. With the unemployment rate near 10 percent, financial institutions taking massive losses, and the government spending trillions of dollars, there is plenty of pain and fear to go around.

It's understandable that so many feel the world as we know it is coming to an end. But the Great Depression experienced an average unemployment rate of 19 percent for a decade (1931–1940) and a string of four years with the jobless rate above 20 percent (1932–1935). Today, the economy is not even close to that type of collapse. About the only thing that really does resemble the 1930s is how politicians and political pundits are using the crisis to gain political advantage.

Probably the most egregious example of this was Paul Krugman's *New York Times* column from May 31, 2009, "Reagan Did It."[1] In his column, he said that the Garn–St. Germain Depository Institutions Act, signed into law by Ronald Reagan way back in 1982, was the "key wrong turn—the turn that made [the current] crisis inevitable."

Krugman claimed that Garn–St. Germain turned "modest sized troubles of savings-and-loan institutions into an utter catastrophe." He tied this to today's crisis by arguing that rising consumer debt levels were "made possible by financial deregulation." Thus, in one fell swoop, he blamed just about everything that has gone wrong in the past 30 years on Ronald Regan.

This is all absolutely absurd. First, Garn–St. Germain—legislation that provided much-needed regulatory relief to savings and loans (S&Ls)—was passed by an overwhelming majority in a Democratically controlled House, 272–91. Then the Senate passed the legislation by voice vote—it was supported so widely that there was no need to count votes.

In the 1970s, S&Ls had their hands tied by three major regulations. First, the interest rates they could pay to depositors were capped at 5½ percent. Second, the only loans they were allowed to make were 30-year fixed-rate mortgages—no adjustable-rate mortgages and no other types of loans. Third, their business was geographically isolated—S&Ls were only allowed to make mortgage loans within a 50-mile radius of their home office.

These regulations set the S&L industry up for collapse. As inflationary monetary policy in the 1970s lifted interest rates above the government's artificial cap, the S&Ls lost depositors to money market funds. The S&Ls then sold certificates of deposit to the money market funds, which meant they were paying market rates to the defecting depositors anyway. At the same time, in the 1970s, many mortgages were assumable, meaning a seller could transfer his mortgage (with the same outstanding loan amount and interest rate) to a buyer. This meant that S&Ls were paying higher rates for deposits than they were earning on loans. In 1982, before Garn–St. Germain was even passed, the S&L industry had a tangible net worth of basically zero.[2]

When Paul Volcker raised short-term rates above 20 percent in the early 1980s, the banking and S&L crisis exploded into an even bigger problem. To blame all this on deregulation, as Krugman does, is simply misdirection. It was not deregulation that caused financial problems, but mistakes in monetary policy that drove inflation and interest rates up, and nanny-state regulation that made it impossible for S&Ls to defend themselves against the economic environment. The banking crisis of the 1980s is a perfect example of government failure, not market failure. And, for that matter, so is the Panic of 2008.

The attempt by Paul Krugman to shift blame to deregulation, and then in a gratuitous fashion to Ronald Reagan, is sleight of hand. But there is a method in his madness. If he and other supporters of big-brother government can convince everyone that capitalism and free markets led to the crisis, then they can rally support for growth in government, which is what they have always wanted.

Intellectually speaking, this attempt at misdirection—at blaming capitalism—is really quite daring. If we apply the logic of the left to airplanes, you can see how ridiculous it is. Airplanes fly partly because wind flowing over and around the wing generates lift. The science behind this dynamic was discovered by Daniel Bernoulli; but when planes crash, no one questions the science of fluid dynamics.

Capitalism is also a natural force. It is an organic method of arranging the economy that has proven itself over centuries. To argue that economic problems occurred because capitalism failed is the equivalent of saying that a plane crashed because Bernoulli's principle doesn't work anymore. But that, of course, can't be true. Capitalism did not fail—it never fails.

The current crisis, just like the Great Depression and the stagflation of the 1970s, has its roots in government policy mistakes. While we all wish the crisis had not happened at all, seeing it as government failure—not market failure—should give us hope for the future. The future looks much brighter than the pouting pundits of pessimism would have you believe.

Fear and Anger Are Understandable

Certainly, some of the most venerable names in U.S. business failed and the stock market was down nearly 60 percent from peak to trough. The housing market collapsed, and the unemployment rate rose to its highest level in 26 years. The government is running budget deficits in the trillions of dollars and is taking over financial firms and auto companies, all the while making very noisy plans to redistribute more and more wealth.

With retirement savings decimated and jobs and houses lost, fear and anger are understandable. Many people just want someone to blame. And there seems to be plenty to go around. So just what is there to be optimistic about?

In my view, a great deal. We are alive during a period of unbelievable technological progress. The combination of technology and entrepreneurship is pushing toward great new inventions right now, as it has for hundreds of years. Productivity is booming, the potential of the Internet has barely been realized, new drugs and medical equipment are being worked on at a frenetic pace, energy research is accelerating (even without government subsidies), and the list goes on and on.

Think about your hobbies—golf, tennis, biking, photography, or model trains. No matter where you turn, new technology is changing everything—for the better. And all of this is lifting living standards and wealth to new heights.

What people think are stumbling blocks are less important than they seem. Human beings have confronted mountain ranges, oceans, pandemics, jungles, panics, depressions, and world wars, yet here we stand. Despite some very serious economic trouble, and many forecasts that the end had come, wealth has continued to expand for 200-plus years. So why *shouldn't* we be optimistic—things have been getting better for a long time, and this is unlikely to change right here and right now.

Just so you don't think I'm crazy, there *are* things that people should worry about. The U.S. economy will pay a long-term price if the government continues to interfere in the marketplace. Capitalism is still the best—and only—way to create long-term increases in wealth, and the more the government moves to redistribute income in a socialist fashion, the more our economic growth could suffer.

But, as of right now, the potential damage from government action has been priced into the market. For at least the next year, probably two, the stock market and the economy will surprise many as they remain resilient and robust in the face of a potential negative drift in government policy. This has happened before, in 1934–1937 and then again in 1975–1976, when the stock market did well despite a negative drift in government policy during these periods.

While many conservatives are terrified about the current populist drift in economic policy, the United States not only survived the 1930s and 1970s, it prospered in the years that followed. Moreover, there were companies and investment strategies that did well in both the 1930s and the 1970s. The United States is a very resilient country.

In order to understand this optimism, it is important to look back at what caused the so-called crisis we have just lived through. It's not what the conventional wisdom tells you. And understanding why the conventional wisdom is wrong is the most important step in overcoming the near brainwashing that our popular press and political class have provided over the past few years.

To be absolutely, 100 percent clear, I do not believe that greed, capitalism, high levels of debt, subprime loans, credit default swaps, derivatives, criminal activity, or leverage were the root problems that caused the Panic of 2008. They may have generated a great deal of fear once the panic started, and they were definitely at the center of the story, but they did not cause the panic.

The United States (and the world) did not experience a failure of capitalism. Nor was it a "failure of finance," as *The Economist* magazine called it.[3] We did not replay the Great Depression, and it wasn't the end of the world. American economic history is filled with economic shocks that were larger and more dangerous than the Panic of 2008.

It was government policy mistakes that pushed the economy to the edge of crisis in the first place. Then, it was government remedies, rules, and regulations (like mark-to-market accounting[4]—enacted just weeks before the crisis became a crisis) that turned a run-of-the-mill problem into a catastrophe. Problems spread, and as the saying goes, "When the tide goes out, you can tell who is swimming naked."

Not only did many financial firms fail, which is understandable, but car companies and newspapers that were already on the cusp of serious financial difficultly were pushed into bankruptcy. There was a combination of a lame-duck Bush administration that believed in government spending and a newly elected populist Obama administration that started throwing around trillions of dollars to "save" the financial system. They forced companies to take government money and demonized the capitalist system. As a result, the government became more entangled in the economy than at any time in American history.

In an ironic twist, some pundits measure the depth and breadth of our economic problems by how much the government spent trying to solve it. Federal Judge and University of Chicago Law Professor Richard Posner put it this way:

> [The recession's] gravity is measured not by the unemployment rate but by the dizzying array of programs that the government is deploying and the staggering amounts of money that it is spending or pledging—almost $13 trillion in loans, other investments and guarantees—in an effort to avoid a repetition of the 1930s.[5]

No matter how smart Richard Posner may be, this argument reflects very poor logic. It is the false logic of *post hoc, ergo propter hoc*—after this, then because of this. If the fire department comes to your house and starts chopping holes in your roof, breaking windows, and pumping water everywhere, then your house is supposed to be on fire. But, in reality, it might not be. Fire department activity alone does not prove anything.

The good news is that the fire department doesn't do this. The fire department has nothing to gain by fighting fires that don't exist. However, the government does have something to gain from creating crisis when there is none. This is not some nefarious, black helicopter thought. It is a simple and straightforward thought based on human nature. Groucho Marx once said, "Politics is the art of looking for trouble, finding it, misdiagnosing it, and then misapplying the wrong remedies."

Politicians want to be seen as savior because it wins votes from those who think the government saved them from some terrible fate, whether the threat was real or not. The government also is very fearful that if it doesn't do something to thwart a perceived problem, it will be blamed if things go wrong. As a result, politicians typically overreact. This is what government does; it grows and acts. Sometimes this is just natural instinct, but sometimes it's the desire of those in control.

Rahm Emmanuel, now President Obama's chief of staff, said last November in the early days of transition between President Bush and President Obama that "You never want to let a serious crisis go to waste. And by that I mean to do things you think you could not do before."[6]

But when the government does this—when it grows and acts—it often makes problems worse, not better. The Great Depression is an example of a problem that was made worse by government action—economic growth was decimated because the government interfered in the market process and acted too radically.

Lately, big-government supporters have been arguing that Herbert Hoover and Franklin Roosevelt didn't spend enough in the Great Depression to lift the economy from its crisis. But Hoover lifted federal outlays from 3.4 percent of gross domestic product (GDP) in 1930 to 6.9 percent in 1932. Roosevelt lifted outlays to 8 percent of GDP in 1933, and an average 10.1 percent of GDP between 1934 and 1936.

But spending is only one measure of government activity. As detailed in *The Forgotten Man* by Amity Shlaes, government meddled in just about every arena of economic activity and became extremely aggressive about attacking and regulating businesses:

> Government management of the late 1920s and 1930s hurt the economy. Both Hoover and Roosevelt misstepped in a number of ways. Hoover ordered wages up when they wanted to go

> down. He allowed a disastrous tariff, Smoot-Hawley, to become law when he should have had the sense to block it. He raised taxes when neither citizens individually nor the economy as a whole could afford the change.
>
> Roosevelt's errors had a different quality but were equally devastating. He created regulatory, aid, and relief agencies based on the premise that recovery could be achieved only through a large military style effort.
>
> Other new institutions, such as the National Recovery Administration, did damage . . . NRA rules were so stringent they perversely hurt businesses. They frightened away capital, and they discouraged employers from hiring workers . . . The resulting hesitation in itself arrested growth.[7]

The good news is that government has shown that it can do the right thing. Contrary to Krugman's point of view, the government behaved in a much better manner during the banking and S&L crisis of the 1980s and 1990s. Between 1980 and 1995, the United States experienced a true financial crisis, with nearly 2,800 banks and S&Ls failing or needing assistance. Despite this, and once the Volcker recessions of the early 1980s were over, the economy prospered, with unemployment falling from 11 percent to 5 percent, while the S&P 500 rose from 102 in 1980 to 616 by the end of 1995—a 500 percent increase.

In that time period, the government did not try to save the day by spending money, cutting interest rates, and taking over financial institutions; it marched to a different drummer. Nondefense government spending (after surging in the recession) was allowed to fall as a share of GDP after 1983. Income tax rates were cut, not hiked. And Paul Volcker at the Federal Reserve held real (or inflation-adjusted) interest rates high to keep inflation low and the dollar strong.

Apparently, government learned nothing from that episode. In the past few years, government spending has exploded, rising from 20 percent to 26 percent of GDP, while the Fed has cut interest rates to near zero. There has been a bipartisan battle cry for government intervention, and it started immediately in August 2007 when financial market problems first appeared. Since then, both Republicans and Democrats, conservatives and liberals, have pushed for more government spending, bailouts, and Fed ease. All of these supporters of government argue that there was no choice, even though it is clear from history there was a choice.

Unfortunately, the alternative choice—to follow free-market, pro-growth, and stable dollar policies like it did in the 1980s—would not grow the government. In other words, this time (as compared to 25 years ago) the government did what it often does and involved itself in a way that made things worse.

All this does not mean that the government has truly killed the goose that lays the golden eggs. Not yet, at least. There is still a vast reservoir of support for free-market capitalism in America. As a sign of this, the May 2009 vote on six ballot measures in California, in the midst of its worst budget crisis in history, showed wide and deep support for lower taxes and less spending. In the end, California's deficit-closing budget, which was finally passed in July 2009, included a heavy emphasis on spending cuts, not tax hikes.

In Illinois, Governor Quinn's 2009 proposal to lift state income tax rates by 50 percent failed miserably in the state legislature. Democratic legislators were scared to vote on a tax hike before the next election. At the same time, the Obama administration found it impossible to break through the bureaucratic logjam and pass cap-and-trade legislation. Health care reform—President Obama's dream to create universal health care in the United States—hit a major roadblock in Congress during the summer of 2009.

And in the midst of all this government activity to "save the world," the economy proved its resilience. In January 2009, while economists were adjusting their forecasts lower to account for what appeared to be a true collapse in global economic activity, U.S. consumers shocked the world and lifted their retail spending by 1.7 percent in one month. Looking back, the economy was already showing signs of a V-shaped recovery when many economists were downgrading their forecasts. The U.S. economy has done this often in the past two centuries.

With the Fed pumping massive amounts of new money into the system and panic subsiding, the economy is set for a surge in growth that will last for the next 12 to 18 months at least. Yes, the path of government policy is problematic for the out years, but for right now things are much brighter than most investors seem willing to contemplate.

History versus Emotion

I know it's hard to believe, in the midst of all of this mayhem, that some good things might actually happen. In fact, there are many who think that acting positive these days is the equivalent of blasphemy.

One of the key ingredients to an optimistic outlook is an ability to think in time, to have a historical perspective. Unfortunately, this is difficult for a great many people. I may sound like an old fogey when I say this, but history has become a boring and meaningless subject to many people. Instead, feelings and emotions seem to have been elevated to the level of truth.

Rightly or wrongly, much of this can be blamed on the ubiquitous nature of the press. This is not the fault of journalists themselves. They are smart people who, if given a chance, could report on history. But they don't have time because they are kept busy responding to the demands of today's audience that we talk about everything that happens as it is happening. This has hurt our willingness, or maybe our ability, to think clearly in the context of history.

Business news is about getting and holding eyeballs, so it tells a story that is easy to follow and very compelling. It often pits the little guy against the corrupt and powerful institutions or people. The most compelling story is the exciting one, with evil businessmen perpetrating some terrible fraud on some unwitting, naïve people.

Think about what makes the regular evening news most nights—murder, crime, flu pandemics, and nasty weather—and how it defines us as helpless victims. Or cable news—which is filled with the drug-induced shenanigans of celebrities or nasty, drawn-out court cases—where human suffering becomes entertainment. While it's not quite as obvious, these are the same audience desires that business news wants to connect with.

This is why business writers and their editors have a deep need to explain every move of every market, every day. As long as the headline says "the market did this *because of that,*" then the story is complete. Never mind that one headline about the bond market uses an interpretation of the data that is exactly the opposite interpretation used in a story about the stock market. As long as there is a reason, and preferably one that fits in a headline or screen scroll, then everyone seems happy.

This leads to confusion. Often, there is no real explanation for market movements, or at least one that is obvious. So if we need to say that the market just did what it did because it's the market, then that's okay. It may not sell many newspapers or gather a big audience, but it's better than making up something and confusing people.

What does sell newspapers is reporting on the outliers. Stories about a wreck on the highway or a house that burns down are very sad stories. But they are outliers. A vast majority (99.9 percent) of car trips are safe and successful. And most houses don't burn down. Imagine the news reporting every morning all the names of people who made it to work on time and safely or all the houses that didn't burn down. Who would watch that?

As it is with almost all news reporting, crime gets reported, while "no crime" is taken for granted; successful international treaties negotiated barely make the news at all, but a breakdown in international affairs gets front page headlines. The news is about reporting what goes wrong, not what is normal or what goes smoothly or what is good. The same is true of economic news. It's not for nothing that the vast majority of business news reporting has been about the excitement of bankruptcy, foreclosure, unemployment, or crime. That's what is exciting.

But the true story of business and economics has been one of consistent, but very slow, progress. Living standards have risen, on average, about 2 percent per year for the past 100 years. The day-to-day story of this progress is about as boring as watching paint dry.

Imagine turning on the business news and seeing a story about how UPS uses mathematical algorithms to determine the most time- and fuel-efficient routes for its delivery trucks. Or that General Electric figured out that it could save money by using voice over Internet protocol (VOIP) telephones at its call centers. Or that a small business owner decided to buy a machine and bring a formerly outsourced service in-house to lower costs and cut prices. Or that an entrepreneur had to forget inventing things for a while so that he could teach young employees how to answer the phone and smile at customers.

I'm not saying that any of this news would be popular, even though it is what business and economic progress is all about. In the world of business journalism, it would probably turn up the snooze meter so high that most people would tune out. The end result is that we end up taking the normal progress of the capitalistic system for granted. The everyday activity of the entrepreneur to deliver goods and services at lower cost and higher quality seem to fly under the radar.

With all this reporting of the outliers—the failures—not the progress, investors, consumers, savers, borrowers, retirees, and politicians get a warped sense of perspective. They bounce from one negative issue to another with no way to tie one thing to the next. Everyone becomes an economist, but for only one issue at a time. As a result, there is no comprehensive story about what is happening, what happened, or how we got to where we are.

To make matters worse, the press is typically an ally of government. This happens for two reasons. First, the press is traditionally liberal. While this book is not the place to "prove" this fact, I have spent a great deal of time with the press in my role as a "talking head," and I have experienced this firsthand.

For the most part, coverage of the economy during the election of 2000, which pitted Al Gore (Clinton's vice president) against George Bush, was positive even though there were clear signs of a slowdown and the stock market was falling fast. The press completely missed, or ignored for as long as it could, the recession of 2001. And when the economy was strong in 2004, during the Bush-Kerry contest, the press was still trying to say the economy was weak. The only explanation that makes sense here is that the press was biased.

Second, the press wants (and needs) access to government officials. As a result, the business press will rarely jeopardize that access by writing critical stories. Reporters who write critical stories can be cut off.

This is made even more damaging by the nature of the relationship between the press and the government. When a high government official, like the secretary of the Treasury, travels to a foreign country, some members of the press are asked to travel along on the government plane. This is a privilege, and the invitation can be withdrawn at the whim of the secretary or the press officer.

For a reporter and his or her career, these trips are extremely valuable. Just like war-zone reporting, these trips help journalists "earn their stripes." Reporting on an important economic visit to a foreign government boosts a business reporter's value in the eyes of his peers, the industry, and the world, and most importantly, his boss.

While war-zone reporting and the White House Press Corps are open to just about every accredited media outlet—rarely is anyone excluded—this is less the case with other government agencies. For instance, with the secretary of the Treasury, there is not a large press pool. Only a select few are invited, and if they report in a negative light, they will most likely be left behind the next time. This absolutely must have an impact on the coverage, and it clearly leads to bias.

When Treasury Secretary Timothy Geithner traveled to China last June, he told a group of Chinese students that "Chinese assets [invested in the United States] are very safe." According to a report in the U.K. *Telegraph*, this provoked "loud laughter from the audience of students."[8]

This story was reported by foreign reporters (including the BBC), but apparently was ignored by the press pool traveling with the secretary. The next day, in Beijing, Timothy Geithner sat down with CNBC reporter and press pool member Steve Liesman for a one-on-one interview. He told Steve that the Chinese were confident about U.S. policies and investments. This seems to be a contradiction, or at least one that ignores the students, but one would have to search the Internet to find that out.

Investors who watch the news uncritically, without running it through a filter to adjust for the biases listed above, make decisions based on a questionable and carefully selected set of facts. So today, for example, the conventional wisdom argues that we have experienced a failure of finance or capitalism. At the same time, many journalists suggest that government intervention has been successful, or at least they do their best to ignore any signs to the contrary.

Buck Up and Remember History

There is no doubt that all of this has had a major impact on the psyche of the average investor. In my travels, which take me all over the world talking with market participants, what I sense is a loss of faith in the future. Many have begun to seriously question whether we can return to "normal." For the first time in nearly 30 years, I sense that many worry that their children will have lower living standards than they themselves have enjoyed.

They shouldn't. The U.S. economy has faced much worse times in the past century, yet it has still grown in 80 out of the past 100 years and 45 out of the past 50 years. During that time, per-capita real GDP has nearly tripled. This puts things in a different perspective. And when it comes down to it, perspective is the key to successful living and investing. What I hope to prove in the rest of this book is that it is not as bad as many people think. In fact, I think the future is still pretty darn bright.

Chapter 2

Capitalism Wins (Again)

It is history—the concept of where we came from—that helps us understand where we are going. And what history tells us is that laissez-faire capitalism and free markets are not dead. They did not cause the crisis, and they won't hinder the recovery. In fact, free-market capitalism is probably the greatest success story of secular human history.

There will be plenty of time to talk about the exact nature of the current financial crisis in the chapters to come. But the place to start in building an optimistic case is to think through the history of free-market capitalism. This is an essential step in understanding what the future holds.

The immense wealth that the U.S. and global economy have built up over the centuries is a key reason for believing that this panic will be short lived. The reservoir of past capital accumulation not only makes recovery more likely and cushions the bottom; it also suggests that the recovery will be stronger and more rapid than conventional wisdom expects.

Some analysts seem to believe that the size and complexity of the economy, and the depth and breadth of the debt markets, make problems more likely and more dangerous. It's almost as if they believe that the more successful we are, the more likely it is that we will fail.

Part of this is because many people see success in a negative light. They seem to believe that sharp increases in wealth, as we have seen in the most recent three or so decades, are false and precarious. For them, success is difficult to comprehend. This notion—that economic growth is unsustainable, unstable, and somehow negative for society—is at the root of a great deal of the pessimism we face today.

Pessimism is a funny thing. Pessimists just can't believe that good times can last. The longer things stay good and the longer the pessimists are wrong, the more they become convinced they will eventually be right. And once something does go wrong, no matter how long they have to wait, the pessimists convince themselves that their long-held beliefs were perfectly legitimate and correct all along.

Demand versus Supply

For economics, much of this negativity and pessimism has it roots in demand-side economic thinking—the belief that economic growth is determined by consumption (demand). This is the opposite of supply-side thinking—the belief that economic growth and wealth creation comes from entrepreneurship, innovation, and creativity.

This is not just a political bumper sticker difference in ideology. Supply-siders do not walk around saying, "Cut taxes and watch it trickle down." Demand-siders do not defend government spending no matter what. They could say or do these things, but their differences are much bigger and deeper than this.

Demand-siders tend to be pessimistic, fret about greed and debt, worry about leaving people behind, think emotion is a driving force behind economic activity, see everything as win-lose, and worry about running out of resources. They tend to believe growth is ephemeral, that consumer spending comes and goes on the wind, but that government can fix any problem when something inevitably goes wrong.

Supply-siders tend to be optimistic, get excited about others' achievements, have faith that people can succeed, believe things can always get better, and believe that progress is real and dependable. While some supply-siders are prone to seeing bubbles in the economy, for the most part they don't blame consumer emotion for them. They blame government policy that artificially stimulates one sector or another. Supply-siders rarely argue for more government intervention.

We would like to think that the differences between these two thought patterns have deep intellectual underpinnings and are based in academic research. But much of the difference in these two types of people is just plain old human nature. For example, it doesn't take an intellectual to stir up fear about running out of resources. Human beings have worried about that for a very long time. However, economists and politicians have taken these ideas and extrapolated them into all kinds of economic theory and government policy.

In fact, the economic policy-maker-in-chief, President Barack Obama, and his economic team are clearly demand-siders. They talk of catastrophe and running out of energy or clean air. And they claim that the only way to save the American economy is for the government to spend money, because people can't or won't. This is a demand-side response and is famously tied to John Maynard Keynes.[1]

Demand-siders look at the world as if it is one giant treadmill of materialism. No wonder they are often so glum. If people stop spending, if people hold back, then the economy is in trouble. If someone else gets there first, there will be nothing left for me. It's all about buying things, getting things, and having things—and things are scarce.

This is where our nation's church pastors enter the fray. They often complain about capitalism because it supposedly encourages people to take their eye off of God and place it on material things. If you believe in the demand-side view of the world, it's easy to believe that materialism makes the world go round.

What's interesting, though, is that no matter how much people complain about materialism and greed, when the economy gets in trouble, the first thing demand-siders want to do is stimulate the buying of things. And in order to do this, they increase government spending or subsidize some activity. To do this, they often tax money from one group and turn right around and give it to another group they think is more likely to spend.

If people are buying fewer houses, the government thinks that by subsidizing housing with tax breaks or by cutting mortgage rates, economic activity will be lifted. If people are saving, then raising taxes and giving the money to someone who doesn't save is proposed.

But, as Milton Friedman said, "There's no such thing as a free lunch."[2] If we need government to move in with guns blazing to artificially lower mortgage rates, then someone will pay. Mortgage holders may pay less today, but lenders will pay a price in the future as they earn interest rates that are artificially low.

While demand-siders think that stimulating demand by taking from one group and giving to another group is a wise policy, they paradoxically also have a zero-sum view of the world. Somehow they hold these two different thoughts in their head at the same time. They think that when the rich get richer the poor get poorer, but they also think that taxing the rich and giving it to the poor (making the rich poorer and the poor richer) somehow helps the economy grow.

President Obama's economic team assumes that raising tax rates will not hurt the overall wealth of the land because it's all one big pot that needs to be stirred. Some liberal economists even believe that redistributing wealth will accelerate economic activity because lower-income people spend more of their income. They truly believe that redistribution lifts economic activity because the poor save less of their income than the rich. And since spending (demand) makes the world go round, we will all be better off if we spend more and save less.

President Obama argues that ". . . with the private sector so weakened by this recession, the federal government is the only entity left with the resources to jolt our economy back to life."[3] Unfortunately, the federal government gets those resources from the private sector in the first place. So where does the "jolt" come from?

Zero-sum thinking does not apply only to money. It is at the root of the arguments about resource scarcity and renewable energy. What most people don't realize is that this argument has been around for hundreds of years (or more). As far back as 1798, Thomas Malthus fretted that there were too many people in the world and not enough food.[4] He's dead and he was wrong—making him a "dead-wrong" economist.

In 1977, President Carter told the world that we were running out of oil. Malthusian economists and geologists convinced him that the price of oil would continue to skyrocket as the world hit peak oil production in the mid-1980s. He's not dead yet, but he sure was wrong.

Supply-siders do not think this way. In fact, even though many of them won't admit it, supply-siders think about things the way our pastors should. After all, pastors tell us that God created human beings in His image. They also tell us that God is a creator. So, in reality, our human interaction on an economic level is not about the treadmill of materialism; it's about the fire of invention, innovation, and creativity. In Latin, the phrase ex nihilo—out of nothing—is used in conjunction with God's creation of heaven and earth.

In the supply-side world, shortages are a call for innovation—for ex nihilo creation. Malthus was wrong because he did not account for technological advances in agriculture. Carter was wrong, too—the world did not run out of oil when he thought it would. Nor did the lights go out when society ran low on whale blubber. Kerosene, the invention of electricity, and the light bulb kept them on. And the most powerful economic force of the past 35 years has been the computer chip, which in essence is made from sand. In other words, human beings have created "something out of nothing."

Supply-siders get excited about the future and remain mostly optimistic because they believe in human ingenuity. They look for ways to encourage risk taking, wonder where the next invention will come from, and believe that opportunity is endless. What the Austrian economist Joseph Schumpeter described as "creative destruction"[5] is the process of economic advancement.

No supply-sider I know enjoys watching people lose their jobs or witnessing industries wither, but they realize that it is inevitable. Moreover, they know that the more government intervenes in the process, the longer the pain will last. There may be an argument for spreading the cost of some economic losses across society as a whole, but the important thing to remember is that this does not erase the loss; it just shifts it onto unsuspecting people who had nothing to do with it in the first place.

And this gets to the root of the matter. As demand-siders run around trying to find ways to support the housing sector, the auto sector, newspapers, and banks, it is supply-siders that remind them that all this support cannot stop the inevitable. The spending must come from somewhere. Every dollar that is shifted by the government from one sector of the economy to another has a cost. The true price of that redistribution is a loss of productive effort somewhere else. This loss of entrepreneurial zeal could come immediately or it may not be seen for years, but it will come.

Demand-siders believe in central control because they have an "add-'em-up" view of economic output. This means demand-siders look at the economy as a combination of spending from all areas. To them, government spending is equal to consumer spending. There is no difference.

Supply-siders follow production. They look at the output of the economy and attempt to measure how entrepreneurs and new inventions will raise productivity and lift living standards. Supply-siders have faith in individuals, especially in crisis, while demand-siders have faith in government.

Ask yourself this question: What is the best way to find gold? Should we parachute the 101st Airborne, generals and first lieutenants, into the California wilderness with picks and shovels, march them around, and order them to find gold? Or should we let 30,000 scruffy, burly, stinky miners loose in the mountains with absolutely no organization? My bet is on the miners. They have their own self-interest in mind. They will all use different techniques and go different places. They are much more likely to be successful.

If you think about this, it is why the private sector is so much better at doing things than the public sector. The U.S. government took over Amtrak in 1970. It still owns Amtrak to this day, and it loses money every year even though it has a monopoly. The U.S. Postal Service, despite its exemption from taxes and its billions in direct subsidies, still has a tough time competing with UPS and FedEx.

The two sectors of the economy with the greatest levels of government intervention are health care and education. Government spends somewhere between 40 and 45 cents of every health care dollar and more than 75 cents of every education dollar. Whenever government gets involved, prices go up and quality falls. No wonder these are the two sectors of our economy that have the most consistent and recognized problems.

General Motors, now known as Government Motors, will likely have the same story to tell in 40 years if the government does not treat it like a private company. If it becomes a politically correct, union-centered, environmentally focused, government-run entity, it will be in for decades of losses.

This movement toward demand-side economic management is a negative and moves the United States away from the supply-side policies that were so successful over the past 25 years. But arguing, or believing, that this move will wreck the economy and that everyone should buy gold, canned goods, and guns is not productive and certainly not profitable.

Economic history seems clear. Throughout the centuries, there have been many attempts to hold back the engine of economic growth—entrepreneurship—but they never work. The supply-side view of the world is not just a theoretical point of view; it's a view that is consistent with human nature. Let's look at how that has turned out.

The History of the World

Angus Maddison, a Scottish professor of economics and preeminent economic historian, has written hundreds of thousands of words about the history of economic growth. To summarize his findings about the past 2,000 years in a sentence would look like this:

> Economic growth and living standards were basically unchanged for 1,800 years, and then things got really, really good.

In Contours of the World Economy (Oxford University Press, 2007) and other books, Maddison presents his lifetime of research. The scope of the data available in these books is breathtaking and just too rich and varied to present here in anything but abbreviated form. Nonetheless, for anyone interested in understanding human struggles to make a better life—what the science of economics is really all about—these books are an invaluable resource.

One thing that immediately becomes clear in Maddison's research is that those of us who walk the earth today owe a deep debt of gratitude to our forefathers and mothers. These people lived in squalor for thousands of years, fought disease and each other, dealt with slavery and hunger, yet survived long enough to propagate a new generation. And those new generations did the same thing, over and over again, with little to show for it until the past 200 years.

As Maddison wrote, "In the year 1000, the average infant could expect to live about 24 years. A third died in the first year of life. Hunger and epidemic disease ravaged the survivors. By 1820, life expectation had risen to 36 years in the west, with only marginal improvement elsewhere."[6]

Due to painstaking research by Maddison and others, a 2,000-year history of gross domestic product, population, and price levels has been calculated for over 99 percent of the world (see Figure 2.1). The data is presented using purchasing power parity—a method that allows incomes and prices to be compared in different countries over time. Maddison summarizes 2,000 years of history in this way: "Over the past millennium (1,000 years), world population rose nearly 24-fold, per-capita income 14-fold, GDP 338-fold. This contrasts sharply with the preceding millennium, when world population grew by only a sixth, and per capita income fell."[7]

This description glosses over a major change in growth rates that Maddison found in the most recent millennium. Within the past 1,000 years there was an 800-year period with slow improvement in living standards, and then the most recent 200-year period, when economic growth experienced what can only be described as a massive acceleration.

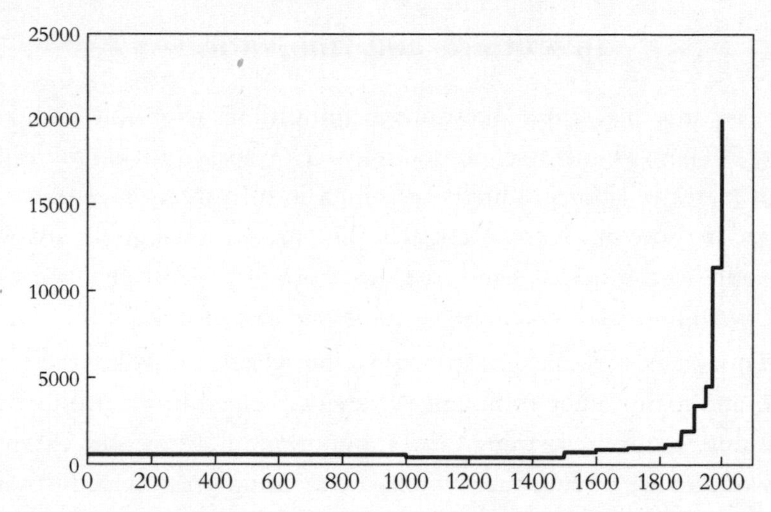

Figure 2.1 Growth Booms in the Past 200 Years: Per-Capita GDP for Western Europe
SOURCE: Contours of the World Economy, 1990 International Dollars

In 1 A.D., the average per-capita income of a citizen of western Europe was $576. One thousand years later, in 1000 A.D., the average per-capita income was just $427. Yes, that's right, because gross domestic product (GDP) growth did not keep up with population growth, per-capita incomes actually fell. Five hundred years after that, in 1500 A.D., incomes had risen to $771 per person, and then 320 years later, in 1820, they had climbed to $1,202. By 1913, in western Europe, per-capita incomes had risen to $3,257 per year, $11,417 in 1973, and $19,912 in 2003 (all income data is expressed in 1990 dollars).

In other words, it took 820 years for incomes to triple after 1000 A.D. They roughly tripled again in the next 100 years: and then they did so again in about 60 years. Since then, in the three decades between 1973 and today, incomes have doubled again.

The second derivative—the change in the rate of change—has been nicely positive since 1500, but especially so since 1820. The question for economists is "why?" Why did growth remain so stagnant for so long? Why did it accelerate? And what does this mean for the future?

Inventions and Innovation

The easy answer to these questions is innovation, invention, and technology. They all increase productivity. The accumulation of capital goods increases labor productivity, which in turn frees up resources to be used in more productive activities. The more capital goods a worker can apply to the task at hand, the more productive his endeavors and the fewer hours that society needs to devote to that task.

Thousands of years ago, spear tips, the wheel, the yoke, the heavy plow, and many other rudimentary devices helped boost productivity in fishing, hunting, farming, and transportation. Eyeglasses extended the working life of craftsmen, while the printing press helped disseminate knowledge more efficiently. Farmers shifted from a two-field to three-field rotation system. And as Maddison pointed out, "Advances in ship design and navigation were the most dynamic form of technical progress from 1000–1820."[8]

But technological progress is only one element of wealth creation. People need more than just inventions. If all it takes is new technology to lift living standards, everyone in the world, except possibly some tribe in a lost land with no access to the modern world, would have seen living standards rise by similar amounts.

Everyone has access to every invention of the middle ages and the industrial revolution. And almost everyone in the world has access to computers, cell phones, automobiles, airplanes, televisions, electricity, and machinery. So, if all it takes to be a successful, wealthy economy is technology, then living standards around the world should be universally high. Unfortunately, they are not.

This has always been true. According to William Easterly, a well-respected expert on economic growth, "The Romans had the steam engine, but used it only for opening and closing the doors of a temple. They even had a coin-operated vending machine, used to dispense holy water in the temple. They had reaping machines, ball bearings, water-powered mills, and water pumps, but did not attain sustained growth."[9]

In the modern era, the Soviet Union found itself in a similar predicament. It sent a man to orbit the earth in a spacecraft before the

United States did so, and was home to some of the most talented scientists (in mathematics, physics, etc.). But all this state-directed talent could not lift living standards. Eventually, the Soviet economy collapsed.

By the way, the Soviet Union creates more headaches for demand-siders. Demand-siders argue that spending is what drives the economy. But people are the same all over the world: in America or Africa today, the Soviet Union in the 1970s, and the Roman Empire 1,500 years ago. All of us have, or had, insatiable demands. Whether it's good health care, electricity, music, or more fuel-efficient cars, no matter what, people always want more. If demand were all it took to create wealth, then there should be no poor country in the world. I have never heard any economist try to make the case that American consumers are better demanders, and that's why the American economy leads the world.

This is because demand alone cannot boost economic activity. And neither can government spending. Despite spending 50 percent of GDP on military budgets, the Soviet Union continued to rot from within, which is exactly what happened to the Roman Empire. That's because wealth is created by entrepreneurs and entrepreneurship, which is lacking today in Africa and was stifled in the Soviet Union and the Roman Empire.

Entrepreneurship

Jean-Baptiste Say is credited with inventing the word entrepreneur. It has its roots in the French word entreprende, which means "to undertake." One textbook says, "An entrepreneur is a person who has possession of an enterprise, or venture, and assumes significant accountability for the inherent risks and the outcome. It is an ambitious leader who combines land, labor, and capital to create and market new goods or services."[10]

The key word in this definition is outcome. The entrepreneur is rewarded by profits for success. It is this profit motive that is the true incentive that encourages people to start businesses or invent new things.

One of the most difficult things to do in the world is start a business. Some estimates suggest that over 90 percent of all new businesses fail within the first few years of operation. It takes a special talent to start a business and keep it running. But entrepreneurs are more than that; they are more than just business managers. A real entrepreneur puts together the resources of the world in a different way (a more efficient way) than anyone else has ever done. Wal-Mart founder Sam Walton pursued one strategy—discounting. He didn't invent retailing, but he revolutionized it, by using every tool he could think of to keep his prices low.

Bill Gates of Microsoft, Gordon Moore of Intel, and Steve Jobs of Apple are all entrepreneurs. They all had different gifts, but they all saw an opportunity to develop a product that would help other people achieve some objective. However, they didn't do this for the rest of us—they did it for themselves. They thought they could profit from what they were doing.

As Ludwig von Mises, who had a true love affair with entrepreneurs, put it in 1956, "Changes in human conditions are brought about by the pioneering of the most clever and the most energetic men. They take the lead and the rest of mankind follows little by little."[11]

This is the key to wealth creation. A successful economy creates an environment where entrepreneurial incentives exist. That environment protects the property rights of the entrepreneur and does not create regulatory handcuffs or subsidize competitors or excessively tax the profits of a successful business. Without incentives, the entrepreneur will be stifled and the economy will not benefit from these people who change the world.

Despite the ability to build an empire and organize great armies, the Roman Empire was a failure at lifting living standards in any significant fashion. Great inventions and technology did not go to waste, but never found widespread enough use to change the way people lived. That's because the environment was not conducive to entrepreneurial activity.

The Turning Point

The turning point for economic success came around 1800. Angus Maddison dates it to 1820. According to Maddison, world per-capita economic growth accelerated from a 0.05 percent rate between 1000 and 1820 A.D, to a rate of 0.54 percent between 1820 and 1870. For the West, growth accelerated from 0.15 percent to 1.07 percent (double the world average), while in America, per-capita growth accelerated from 0.36 percent to 1.34 percent (more than double the world average).

At the beginning of the 1800s, America lagged its western European counterparts in productivity and per-capita income. But, by the 1870s, America had surpassed western Europe, becoming the world leader—a position it has yet to relinquish. However, both western Europe and the United States separated themselves from the rest of the world in the early 1800s—generating much more rapid increases in living standards.

Angus Maddison ascribes this turning point to four factors:[12]

1. Development of secular knowledge and science—a new awareness of human capacity to transform the forces of nature through rational investigations and experiment.
2. The emergence of important urban trading centers was accompanied by changes that fostered entrepreneurship and abrogated feudal constraints on the purchase and sale of property during the 11th and 12th centuries.
3. The adoption of Christianity as a state religion in 380 A.D. led to changes in the nature of many laws like marriage, inheritance, and kinship.
4. The emergence of a system of nation-states in close propinquity, which had significant trading relations and relatively easy intellectual interchange in spite of their linguistic differences. It stimulated competition and innovation.

While these four items include reference to property rights, entrepreneurship, competition, and world trade, Maddison avoids any direct comments on democracy or free markets. This is a safe place for any researcher to hang out. It avoids any direct political battles over socialism versus capitalism.

However, one reason that Maddison can take this position is that his data speaks very loudly. For 1,000 years, in a feudal, state-dominated world, living standards did not improve. Then, between 1000 and 1500, world GDP growth accelerated slightly to about 0.15 percent annually. This barely kept up with population, but it was an acceleration of growth rates. And this corresponded with adoption of the Magna Carta Libertatum (the Great Charter of Freedoms) in 1215, the precursor of the U.S. Constitution.

The Magna Carta codified a belief in the individual and the rule of law and limited the powers of the king. By 1500, feudalism was basically dead.[13] And in 1500, growth rates of GDP accelerated to 0.32 percent, double what they were in the previous 500 years, and then tripled again between 1820 and 1870 to 0.94 percent. For the United States, real GDP growth rates rose from an average 0.86 percent between 1500 and 1820 to 4.2 percent between 1820 and 1870.

This sharp acceleration in world real GDP growth rates (and especially American growth rates) occurred at the same time the United States adopted the Constitution, which placed in one document the protections necessary for a successful entrepreneurial economy. Entrepreneurs cannot "strut their stuff" in an environment that is not free. The Constitution not only provided that freedom, but also described a mechanism for maintaining it and protecting individuals from the power of the state.

Capitalism Wins—It's Not Over

This history is incontrovertible. But the press and their post-modern audience are willing to ignore history because of a weird and somewhat narcissistic tendency to think that whatever is happening right now is the greatest, most important thing that has ever happened. It seems many people believe that only if they are alive during very important times is their life worthwhile.

This leads some to believe that the Panic of 2008 and the election of Barack Obama signal a historic shift in the direction of government policy and capitalism. And, because of this belief, there are many conservative talk show hosts, writers, analysts, and authors, who are convinced that capitalism is dead, gone, buried.

But the momentum of the past 1,000 years, and the relentless pressure on governments and people to move toward freedom, has not ended. The entrepreneurial spirit, and the rules and laws that are in place to support it, are difficult or impossible to dampen or change. Moreover, the idea that capitalism and our economy are fragile enough to be knocked out by the recent financial crisis and panic reveals a misunderstanding of both history and capitalism itself. Entrepreneurship makes an economy more stable, not less.

Every action of an entrepreneur is designed to limit risk and boost the odds of success. Gamblers take risk; entrepreneurs work to eliminate it. The combined impact of billions of decisions, over hundreds of years, has created a very robust and resilient economy and institutional framework. Not only can it withstand crisis, but it would take relentless political effort, over many years, even decades, to tear it apart.

Yes, recent developments in the economy and in the political arena are worrisome and bothersome. But it is better to have faith in what we have built over the past centuries than to doubt it. Faith has proven more correct than fear. Capitalism has always won.

Chapter 3

Creative Destruction

Despite the success of capitalism at lifting living standards, the trials and tribulations of growth and change are still painful. This pain can often lead people to wrong conclusions about the health of the economy. And the perfect example of this is the failure of General Motors and Chrysler in the midst of the Panic of 2008.

With oil prices more than doubling between late 2007 and mid-2008 to $145 per barrel, vehicle sales fell sharply. Then, when Lehman Brothers failed in September 2008 and panic struck, consumers pulled back everywhere and the bottom fell out. Domestic car and truck sales plummeted to just 6.4 million units at an annualized rate by February 2009. This was the lowest number of domestic vehicle sales since the bottom of the recession in 1981, when the population of the United States was just 230 million, or 30 percent less than today. In 2000, domestic automakers sold 14.5 million cars and trucks, nearly two and one-half times the sales pace of early 2009.

Foreign sales add about half again to the total. So total vehicle sales (domestic and foreign) were just 9 million units at an annual rate in early 2009. At this sales pace, the United States wasn't even replacing scrapped (wrecked or just worn-out) vehicles, and it would take 26 years to replace the entire fleet of 240 million vehicles on American roads. No one except a collector drives a car that is more than 26 years old.

No wonder the car companies went under. But even if this jump in oil prices and economic panic had not taken place, General Motors was on its way to the junkyard, or at least to the dry docks for a major overhaul. Its cost structure was frozen in the 1970s—an era of lower productivity growth, higher employment, and strong labor unions. It couldn't last, and it didn't.

GM was removed from the 30-stock Dow Jones Industrial Average on the same day it declared bankruptcy and was replaced by Cisco Systems, Inc. The technology giant Cisco, led by level-headed CEO John Chambers, provides the hardware for a great deal of the world's communication infrastructure.

On its face, this switch in the Dow is a perfect example of Schumpeter's "creative destruction." What used to create profits and economic growth in the past gives way to the new. As technology changes, so does the economy. Just as the agrarian economy gave way to the manufacturing economy as the source of wealth in the industrial revolution, the manufacturing economy is now giving way to technology.

This transformation uproots everything. It is true change. And change is painful. But getting upset about this process is the equivalent to getting upset about aging. As we get older, things don't work as well as they did when we were younger. But along with the downside is an upside. We are wiser for our children, we have experience, we can take advantage of opportunity, we know ourselves better and have deeper friendships, and most people learn how to handle situations better.

This is not a perfect metaphor because the economy doesn't have a life expectancy. And having to wear glasses is not the same as losing your job at 50 because a computer can handle it better. But if we can step back and look at this process from a macro point of view, from 50,000 feet, the process is similar.

Globally, there have been more business starts in the past quarter century than in any other 25-year period in history. So, while many firms find themselves in trouble, new opportunities have expanded dramatically. Yes, destruction is taking place, but creation is as well. Investors and workers who can tell the difference, or just recognize that there is a difference, will benefit handsomely.

The Big "X"

Back in the late 1990s, many people thought that technology would save the Big Three. Ford Motor Company and General Motors even promised to use Internet-based supply-chain management systems to save billions and pass the savings on as profits to the bottom line and shareholders.[1]

This promise was never fulfilled because these types of savings, in competitive industries, are passed right along to the consumer. New technology that is available to one company is almost always available to all companies. As a result, if all car companies can save billions per year with better supply-chain management, then at least one of them will lower prices to gain market share. And once one company lowers prices, they will all be forced to cut prices. If they don't, they will see their sales and profits fall.

The only way to make outsized profits is to provide a higher-quality or more attractive product than your competitor can. By selling something that no one else can sell, whether because of patent protection, great marketing, a focus on quality, or great customer service, companies make profits that their competitors can't. But to do this, the company can't rest. Profits go to the one in the lead.

General Motors did this well for decades. In fact, the success of GM put many other companies out of business—other car companies for sure, but also buggy whip manufacturers, blacksmiths, and even saddle makers. But then history caught up. And while some blame an insular management, or just plain old arrogance, the real problem was that it ran out of energy as it was bogged down by a 100-year old bureaucracy and labor union demands. Health care costs alone added more than $1,000 to the cost of each car produced. GM made promises in a bygone era that it just could not keep in the new world.

One of the real problems with heavily unionized companies is that management has few tools for incentivizing workers. In union shops, the worker takes his or her lead from the union and thanks the union for a raise, not management. The whole process creates stress and strife within the company. In nonunion shops, managers can use promotions and pay increases to direct the effort of workers toward goals or a new vision. If done in the right way, this engenders loyalty and hard work and it is easier to steer the company in a new direction.

This fundamental issue with unions becomes a real problem when technology and transformation accelerate. Productivity growth, when combined with competition, means that companies will shed jobs over time. This is more difficult for unionized companies, and those that do not keep up with productivity improvements and cost cutting get left behind.

They say a picture is worth a thousand words, and Figure 3.1 is proof. It shows industrial production back to 1950 versus total manufacturing jobs as a percentage of the U.S. workforce. This big "X" is a one-picture history of creative destruction, otherwise known as progress. Manufacturing output, as measured by the Federal Reserve, has increased fourfold since 1950. At the same time, total jobs in manufacturing have fallen from 30 percent of the workforce to less than 10 percent.

The United States has fewer manufacturing employees today (12 million) than it did in 1950 (14 million), yet it produces vastly more goods. The jobs have moved to services, where employment (excluding government) is now 91 million versus 22 million in 1950.

Many view the loss of manufacturing jobs as an indication of something wrong with the American economy, when in reality it is just a sign of progress. The loss of manufacturing jobs is a result of massive gains in productivity and creative destruction. It's a good thing, not a bad thing. This tsunami of transformation has occurred around the world. Even China has lost manufacturing jobs.

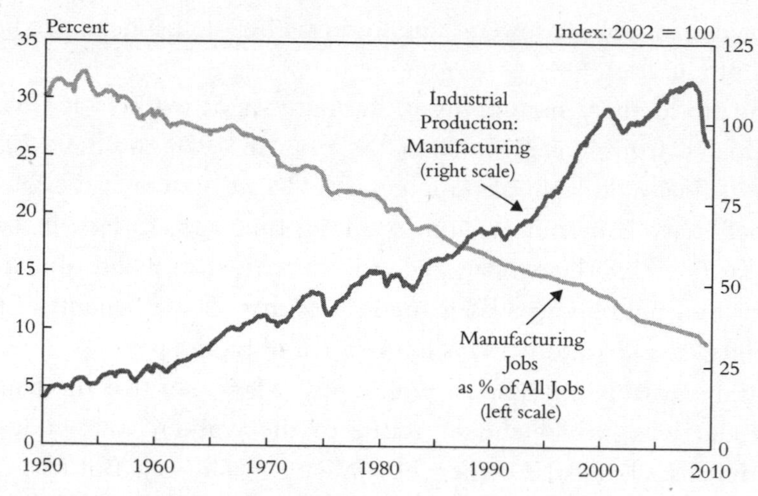

Figure 3.1 Factory Output versus Employment
SOURCE: Federal Reserve Board, BLS

Don't get me wrong—this is a painful process. You can imagine Detroit-area men and women saying, "My grandfather and father worked for GM and they were members of the United Auto Workers; I want this, too." But what they are finding out is that this lifestyle—the one where workers who did not go to college can earn $80,000 or more per year (in today's dollars), have a house, boat, and maybe even a fishing cabin up north—does not exist anymore. And they are devastated. And when there is this much disappointment in the world, people start looking for someone to blame.

Some economists have called it a breakdown in the American dream. They argue that back in the 1950s and 1960s America made an implicit contract with its laborers. They could be paid handsomely for repetitive and boring work, the profits would be spread more evenly, and the American Dream would be available to everyone. Some of these economists now argue that management became greedy and this contract broke down and is no longer valid.

But nothing could be further from the truth. The breakdown has nothing to do with the pitting of one class of people against another. This is just a political argument designed to foster class warfare and the support of one system of government over another. Rather, the loss of manufacturing jobs has everything to do with real change in the process of production.

As productivity has improved, the number of workers at GM has plummeted from over 395,000 at the peak in 1970 to about 70,000 when it finally declared bankruptcy. If GM had not cut its workforce, it would have gone out of business a long time ago. In fact, it should have far fewer workers today, and at lower pay, than it did. But it was caught in a bind because labor unions felt that all the benefits of productivity should go to workers in the form of higher pay.

In a way, this is a Marxist philosophy. Marx said that the benefits of productivity, which should accrue to the worker, were stolen by the capitalist class—the owners of land and machinery. But Marx was wrong. The benefits don't accrue to the capitalist; the benefits accrue to the consumer through lower prices. Both the laborer and the capitalist are consumers. So, as prices fall, living standards rise for the laborer, the capitalist, and all the customers of the business.

But the market is a perfect democracy and a harsh taskmaster. Every day, consumers vote with their dollars. And what consumers want are high-quality products at low prices. As productivity improves, the prices of goods and services fall, but not all capitalists are able to increase productivity at the same pace.

As a result, only those that lead the pack survive. Only the companies that stay on the cutting edge are able to remain profitable. A capitalist who decides to underpay workers and take advantage of consumers by charging higher prices must come to grips with changing technology and his competitors' willingness to cut prices and pay higher wages as productivity improves. His profits are determined by the marketplace, not his greed.

The Industrial Revolution

What better example of this is there than farming? A family farm, one could say, is the capitalist and laborer all wrapped in one person. The farmer owns the land and labors on it to produce food for others to eat. The farmer reaps what he sows and takes the market price for his goods. A farmer can't underpay or overpay himself; he can only take what the market and the weather offer. If the weather does not cooperate, the farmer blames God or fate. If the markets don't cooperate, the farmer often blames other people, and at the turn of the last century farmers were complaining bitterly about what the market offered. As new technology proliferated, and productivity improved, crop prices fell. And those farmers who did not employ the latest technology, who still tried to farm the same way their grandfathers and fathers had, on the same plots of land, could not keep up.

Look at Figure 3.2. It's exactly the same chart as we saw with manufacturing, about a century before, but for farms. In 1880, 49 percent of the labor force were farmers. By 1930 this was down to just 21 percent, but those farms produced many times more than they did in 1880. This is the classic productivity "X" chart that we see in so many industries: more output with fewer inputs.

As productivity improved on the farm and prices fell, those farmers who allowed the momentum of history to bog them down, continuing to farm in the traditional way, saw their profits diminish rapidly. When this happened, many of those farmers who became less profitable looked for something or someone else to blame. In a

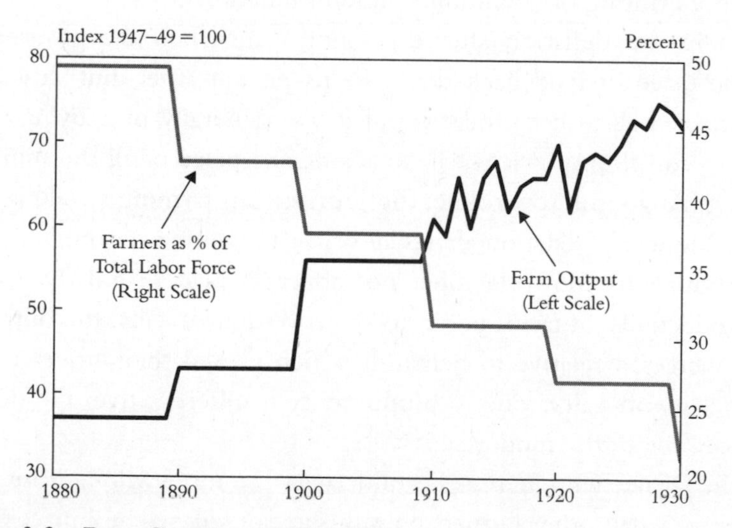

Figure 3.2 Farm Output versus Farmers
SOURCE: Historical Statistics of the United States

democracy, this willingness to blame others leads to political pressure for some kind of change.

In the United States at the turn of the last century, that political pressure led to the formation of the populist political movement. By defending farmers, William Jennings Bryan became one of the movement's leaders. In one of his most famous speeches, he complained bitterly that the "idle holders of idle capital" were hurting the "struggling masses."

This speech, known as the "Cross of Gold" speech, was given at the 1896 Democratic National Convention in Chicago. Bryan said, "Burn down your cities and leave our farms, and your cities will spring up again as if by magic. But destroy our farms and the grass will grow in the streets of every city in the country." What Bryan wanted was an end to the gold standard, which he and others blamed for the falling prices of farm products.

The gold standard is a "hard" money standard. It allows the money supply to increase only as new gold is found or accumulated through trade. There was no Federal Reserve in 1896; therefore, the amount of gold in the system and the rate of exchange determined by the government determined the level of prices. And because this system did not allow the printing of new money, it kept inflation at bay.

There was deflation after the Civil War, when the government put the price of gold back down to its prewar level, but this deflation affected all prices similarly and it was generally over by 1879. In other words, if crop prices fell, so would the price of all the inputs to farming. As a result, over time, the profits from farming would remain intact. Monetary deflation affects all prices the same over the long run.

Productivity, however, does not affect all prices similarly. And as the productivity of farms began to improve dramatically, the output of crops increased relative to demand, which caused their prices to fall. The decline in prices due to productivity is different than the decline in prices due to the money supply.

The farmer who increases productivity the most will increase profits relative to all other farmers because he can still sell at a price above production costs. The farmer who does not increase productivity at all will see profits diminish because his cost of production does not decline. What Bryan was calling for was more money so that inflation would increase crop prices. He wanted inflation.

However, "soft" or "easy" money would have never fixed the problems faced by farmers who still wanted to farm the old way. If inflation were greater than productivity, it would have raised the prices of their products in the marketplace. But seed, land, and all the other inputs that farmers need to grow and harvest crops would have also risen. Inflation does not alter the fundamental process of creative destruction.

As technology altered the fundamental nature of farming, the fabric of society was changed radically. It was painful. Just like the GM workers of the late 20th century, you can hear farmers of the early 20th century saying, "My grandfather farmed this way on this plot of land and so did my father: I want this for my family, too." But this was not to be. Farmers were forced to move their families to the city and take jobs in the factories.

As a sign of how painful this process has been, and how long it has dragged on, Willie Nelson hosted his latest "Farm Aid" concert in October 2009. What is ironic is that it was a financial crisis caused by the inflation of the 1970s that was the final straw for the traditional family farm. Too much leverage and a dependence on rising crop prices caused tumult when inflation ended and crop prices fell in the 1980s. Just like for GM, it was a financial crisis *initially caused by inflationary monetary policy* that wrote the last chapter for farming in the "old way."

The Call for Change

In short, we are living through a turbocharged transformational process that we see only once in a century, or once every two or three generations. The rate of change is astounding and is unsettling for many. It undermines what many people have taken as a way of life that would never change.

This, I believe, was the real push behind the populist candidacy of our current president, Barack Obama. In an ironic twist, his call for change was made in a period where people were living with nothing *but* change. The classic "X" of every industry is a perfect picture of creative destruction—the endless pursuit of a better way.

The problem for most people is that they don't like change that they can't try to control or think they control. As a result, there is a bias toward believing that change caused by entrepreneurs, technology, and markets is chaotic and unfair, while many believe that politically controlled change creates a more "socially just" outcome. Unfortunately, this is a mistake; politically controlled change often creates more pain because it leads to less growth.

In my reading of history, it was Bryan's (and others') call for an end to the gold standard that produced the necessary environment for the creation of the Federal Reserve in 1913. Since that point, the United States has experienced far more inflation than it would have experienced without the Fed. And no matter how much inflation the Fed created, or how many concerts Willie Nelson did, the family farm could not be saved. Today, just 2 percent of Americans work on a farm.

While some people believe that there is a "good" level of inflation that provides grease for the wheels of the economy, this is like believing there is an "appropriate" level of drugs in the system that make things "feel" better. Inflation undermines the value of assets and money and distorts decision making. While many people believe that the United States has been basically inflation free for the past 20 years, the consumer price index shows that what costs $1 today could have been bought for 58 cents in 1989. In other words, the house you bought for $100,000 in 1989 would need to be worth $172,000 today just to keep up with the rising price of goods and services.

If this is what can happen to the value of money in a "low inflation" environment, imagine what happens if we let inflation creep higher. At 5 percent inflation, prices would double every 14 years. This would undermine the value of savings and erode the real value of assets. Inflation does not help anyone.

And while many in government seem to believe that its takeover of General Motors, or its push to regulate health care, or its desire to raise taxes will alleviate the pain of creative destruction, there is absolutely no proof of that at all. The transformation toward more capital-intensive manufacturing processes will continue no matter what the government does. And this will happen in every country around the world.

So what should politicians do about the economic pain that comes from creative destruction and globalization? The answer is not the reason for this book, but we must always realize that real opportunity comes from dynamic growth, not from government handouts. The more the government intervenes in the economy, the more it tries to lessen the pain, the less job growth and the more pain an economy experiences.

In the 15 years between 1993 and 2007, the average unemployment rate in the United Kingdom, Canada, Germany, Italy, and France was 8.2 percent, while the average unemployment rate in the United States was 4.9 percent. Yes, these European countries and Canada have national health care and generous unemployment benefits, but they also have less entrepreneurship and much more unemployment. That's the trade-off. You can't get one without the other.

While people want to be protected from the pain of change, government attempts to do so impede economic activity. Raising tax rates on the successful and profitable and subsidizing the less successful is a recipe for slower growth. The intentions to lessen pain are good and honorable, but the outcome is more pain and less opportunity.

A Wrong Drift, but a Cool Wind

History is clear. The creative destruction signified by the "X" is positive. It leads to progress and better living standards as long as government gets out of the way and lets it happen. Those families who left farms at the turn of the century and moved to the city to work in a factory could not believe that life would be better. But, eventually, they saw this process work. The benefits became visible within a generation.

Economically speaking, farmers' children, grandchildren, and great grandchildren all had more productive lives as a result. They weren't the same "down-home, family-farm" lives; they were different. Some may think this was wrong and bad, but from an earnings point of view, the process worked. Children became more productive than their mothers and fathers. Faith in this process is difficult to keep sometimes, but faith is what we must have.

Unfortunately, the government seems to be singing from the wrong hymnal. Rather than doing things that help the *creative* side of the equation, they are following a path that supports the *destructive* side. By attempting to maintain the status quo, by trying to subsidize and bail out the auto companies, the United States government is supporting the past. To do this, it is shifting resources toward the auto industry and away from other sectors. The government will claim that this is a "third way"—not capitalist, not socialist, but a partnership between government and business.

But there is no such thing as a third way. You can't be a little pregnant. You either are or you are not. Any deviation from the capitalist process of creative destruction, any interference in the process, is by definition anticapitalist.

The government does not have a money tree—it prints, borrows, or taxes all the money it needs to fulfill its side of the transaction. But printing money creates inflation, while borrowing and taxing subtract resources from other, more successful sectors of the economy. Government allocation of resources is, by definition, socialism.

The benefits of this activity accrue to highly visible groups of people—like GM employees—while the costs are borne by a group of people that is basically invisible. A Detroit-area auto worker has his or her job saved, but because the cost of government drains resources from the economy, Seattle will have to do with one less hairstylist. The hairstylist who is not able to find a job is never aware that the cost of government bailouts has reduced demand for services thousands of miles away.

Imagine a GM worker who saw the writing on the wall 15 years ago, quit his highly paid union job, and started his own auto-body repair shop. Now he makes $250,000 per year and has 15 employees. The government calls him "rich" and tells him that he must pay higher taxes to pay for health care and retirement for his old workmates at GM who have lost their job. This isn't fair. In fact, it could cause job cuts or less hiring at his body shop, which would hurt anyone from GM looking for a new job.

Putting this aside, the impact from the GM takeover will be small. While a major name in business, and key focus of labor unions, GM is just not that big, relatively speaking. After the government takeover, there will be roughly 38,000 employees—or just 0.03 percent of all jobs in America. Cisco has 66,000 employees, Microsoft has 91,000, and Wal-Mart has 2.1 million. And to put this in a different perspective, Amtrak had 18,000 workers in the mid-1970s, which was 0.02 percent of all jobs in America.

The economy survived, even thrived after the 1970s, and it actually experienced a boom in 1975 and 1976. Capitalism is very difficult to hold down. And despite the Panic of 2008, the economy is as dynamic today as it has ever been. Productivity is growing strongly, and new inventions are sprouting up on a daily basis.

The dynamism of the economy is often underestimated because economic data is typically focused on net additions or losses. For example, in 2008, the economy lost 2.2 million jobs on a net basis. But if we look underneath this statistic, we find that the economy actually lost over 30 million jobs, but at the same time created roughly 28 million. New businesses are born and die all the time. Projects are started and ended all the time. So to say that the economy did not create any jobs in the past year is just not true. It created tens of millions of new jobs. In recessions, job losses exceed job gains, and as the recovery unfolds in the year ahead, more jobs will be created than lost. It happens every time.

Inflation, Creative Destruction, and the Crisis

Mark Twain is credited with saying, "History does not repeat itself, but it sure does rhyme." And what has traced out a rhyming pattern in recent years is that productivity improvements in the late 1990s led to fear of deflation and demand for more inflationary monetary policy.

Just like the farmers at the turn of the last century complained about deflation and the gold standard, manufacturers were asking for easy money in the late 1990s. Jerry Jasinowski, chief economist for the National Association of Manufacturers, said in March 1999, "[deflation is] a big deal now. . . . Falling prices will cut into profits. . . . Companies have two choices: increase productivity or downsize."[2] This was a consistent theme of Jasinowski's throughout the 1990s.

He finally got his wish after the stock market crashed and deflation fears spread to the mainstream. The Fed then cut interest rates dramatically between 2001 and 2004—to 1 percent. But these rate cuts did not help in the way Jasinowski hoped. Manufacturing continued to lose jobs relative to other sectors of the economy as productivity continued to boom. Oil prices went up, which lifted the cost of production for manufacturers. Moreover, it was this major shift in monetary policy and super low rates that set the stage for overinvestment in housing and the financial panic that has affected the world.

The crash from that overinvestment—the Panic of 2008—happened in the midst of a technological revolution just like the Great Depression hit in the midst of the industrial revolution. As a result, what was already a time of populist sentiment has been exaggerated, and it has become easy for many to believe that the system has come unglued. Many were walking on eggshells already, only to be pushed over the edge by the financial panic.

The government has taken advantage of this and gone wild. As a result, the markets priced in the possibility of another Great Depression. It is highly doubtful that anything remotely like the Depression will occur, partly because the Fed has lowered interest rates to near zero. That means there are tremendous opportunities available for those who can look at what appears to be chaos from a different perspective than the conventional wisdom.

Chapter 4

A Government-Sponsored Recession

One thing is for certain: When the complaints start, only a few people will stand up and say, "It's my fault." As we all know, the one who bears the brunt of the blame for a problem is often the one who doesn't speak up quickly enough, or the one who can't be heard through the din of finger pointing and excuses, or the one who doesn't have the power to stand on a bully pulpit.

As a perfect example of this, imagine Alan Greenspan were still chairman of the Federal Reserve. He would not have to resort to writing op-eds in the *Financial Times* to proclaim his innocence of any misdeeds in the current crisis. He could use the bully pulpit offered by his position, and the press would provide cover because they were interested in being fed scoops about potential changes in Federal Reserve policy or thinking that only he could offer.

If Greenspan were still at the Fed, Treasury Secretary Timothy Geithner could have never thrown him under the bus like he did in an interview with Charlie Rose. In that May 6, 2009, PBS interview, Geithner took aim at the role easy money had in our current problems:

Mr. Rose:	"Looking back, what are the mistakes and what should you have done more of? Where were your instincts right, but you didn't go far enough?"
Mr. Geithner:	"We need a little more time to get full perspective."
Mr. Rose:	"Right."
Mr. Geithner:	"But I would say there were three types of broad errors of . . . policy both here and around the world. One was that monetary policy around the world was too loose too long. And that created this just huge boom in asset prices, money chasing risk. People trying to get a higher return. That was just overwhelmingly powerful."

Geithner tried to give Greenspan a break later in the interview, but the damage was done. It was probably the final pinprick in the Greenspan bubble of infallibility. There were some private-sector economists and journalists who argued as far back as 2001 that the Greenspan Fed was running a monetary policy that was too loose. But the vast majority of commentators went along with the Fed and with just about anything Alan Greenspan wanted to do. Only in retrospect, and without him in power, is an alternative story able to fight its way to the forefront.

The fact that the Fed was "too loose for too long" explains a great deal of the financial crisis we have been living through. Monetary policy is a very powerful force for good or bad. Few truly understand its power. But, because the Fed controls the money supply and, through it, short-term interest rates and the value of the dollar, it affects all decisions that have a price tag. In short, the Fed constructs the glasses that we look through when we make financial decisions.

If the Fed holds interest rates artificially low, then it creates a mirage, where debt financing appears less expensive than it is in reality. As a result, people buy bigger houses than they can afford and financial institutions employ more leverage than they should. In other words, people going about their daily business can be fooled into thinking that they are making good decisions when they are actually making very risky ones.

The bottom line is that government policy creates many more problems than most people ever understand. But when government does damage, it is often able to blame someone else. And because government is able to deflect blame onto corporations and the private sector, many of its mistakes never register in the mainstream media or with the public. What does register is that the system of capitalism can't be trusted. This may help government, but it certainly doesn't help the country.

According to the 2009 Edelman Trust Barometer, 77 percent of media-attentive Americans trust business less this year than they did last year. Overall trust in business fell from 58 percent last year to 38 percent in 2009, the lowest in the barometer's tracking history of 10 years.[1] This is unfortunate. A real understanding of what has happened puts the blame squarely on the government. My best guess is that 90 percent of the factors that led to the housing crisis and the Panic of 2008 can be laid at the feet of politicians, bureaucrats, and Fed policy makers.

If we spend some time looking at the crisis from the ground up, it becomes clear that the capitalist system is still trustworthy. As a result, there are some fabulous opportunities for those who are able to ignore the conventional wisdom. The economy is not broken, and the recovery will be much more robust than most consider possible right now. This means that stock prices have been unfairly beaten up, and that risk is overpriced. To understand why this is so, why this is a panic that will end reasonably quickly and not another Great Depression, it is important to understand what really went wrong.

The Housing Boom

While we could probably go back much further into history, for the sake of brevity let's trace the roots of the most recent housing boom back to 1997. That was when President Clinton and Congress changed the tax rules for housing. Up until the tax bill of 1997, a homeowner was allowed an once-in-a-lifetime tax-free capital gain of $150,000 on the sale of a home. In order to avoid paying taxes, a homeowner could "roll over" the gains from a home sale into a new home as long as the new home was purchased within six months of selling the old one.

Under the new capital gains tax law, homeowners could take $250,000 in tax-free capital gains ($500,000 for a couple) on any home that was a permanent residence for at least two years. When combined with the fact that mortgage interest and real estate taxes can be deducted from income for federal tax purposes, housing became the least taxed investments that a person could make.

The Clinton tax change hit just as baby-boomer parents needed and wanted to move from their suburban homes to condos in the city or retirement homes on a lake. What was already likely to be a robust period for housing activity was turbocharged by this shift in the tax code. Not only did home sales accelerate in 1997, but they remained robust right through the recession of 2000–2001 (see Figure 4.1).

Don't take this the wrong way. These Clinton-era tax cuts (which also included cuts in capital gains taxes for other investments) were a very positive development. But, like all tax cuts, they helped attract resources to a specific sector of the economy (in this case, housing), that might not have gone in that direction otherwise. This helped lift home prices and housing activity above what would have normally occurred.

And then, when the Fed cut interest rates 11 times in 2001, it was like throwing gasoline on a fire. Housing sales took off, and prices rose rapidly. Low tax rates and low interest rates were a major accelerant for housing activity (see Figure 4.1).

In 1995, residential construction represented 4.1 percent of gross domestic product (GDP). In 2002, residential construction was

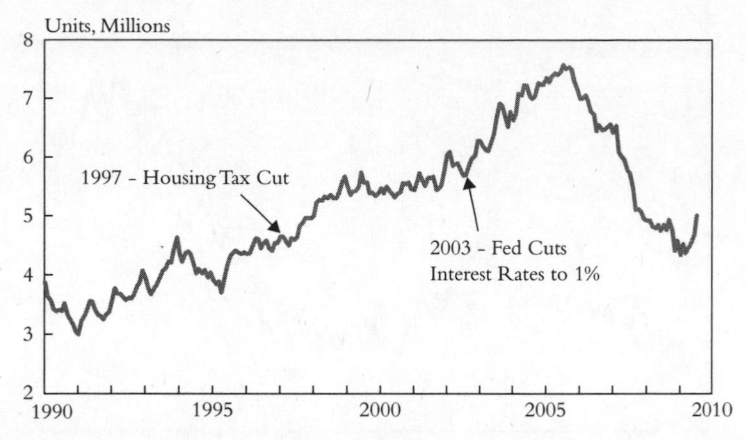

Figure 4.1 Housing Sales, New Plus Existing
SOURCE: Census Bureau, National Association of Realtors

4.8 percent of GDP, but by 2005 it had climbed to an average of 6.1 percent of GDP—a level not seen since the building boom after World War II. Real GDP grew at an average annual rate of about 3.6 percent per quarter from mid-2003 to mid-2005, but just 3.2 percent without housing.

This building boom lifted the percentage of Americans who owned a home from 64 percent in 1994 to 69 percent in 2004—the highest homeownership rates in U.S. history (see Figure 4.2). This increase of five percentage points in just 10 years was probably too much. The only way to do this was to push the edge of the financial envelope, making ownership available to people who might not have qualified in previous years.

It seems clear that the housing market had reached a point that was very precarious. But was it, as many think today, at a point that threatened all of Western civilization and the whole concept of capitalism? Looking at the actual facts makes it really difficult to make that case.

The Crisis Begins

Alan Greenspan put an actual date on the crisis, saying in a speech in late 2007, "The financial crisis that erupted on August 9, 2007, was an

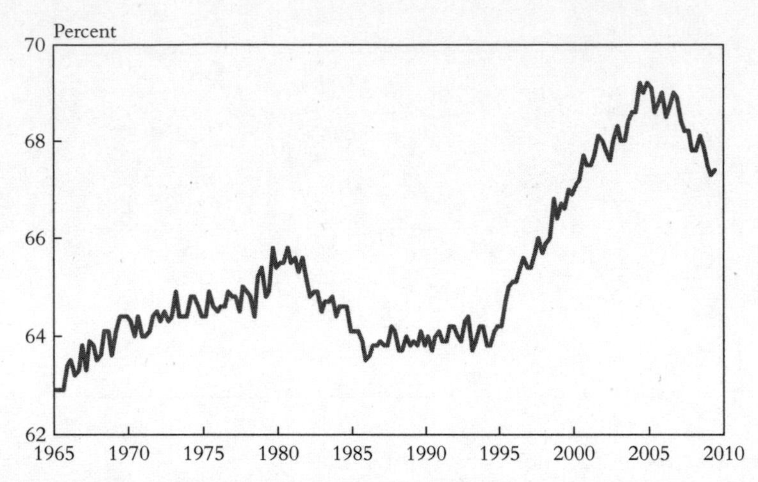

Figure 4.2 Homeownership Rate (% of Population)
SOURCE: Census Bureau

accident waiting to happen."[2] just a few months later, in December 2007, the National Bureau of Economic Research (NBER) says that the recession started.

After looking closely at what happened, two things are clear. First, outside of housing, the recession did not begin until fall 2008 after Lehman Brothers failed. Second, the recession could have been avoided altogether, or minimized greatly, if government had just done things differently.

To understand this, it is important to realize that the housing market actually peaked way back in 2005. In July 2005, new single-family homes sold at a rate of 1.389 million units, up 45 percent from just 36 months before and more than double the sales level of 1995. Existing home sales hit a peak sales rate of 7.25 million units at an annual rate in September 2005, up 30 percent from sales volumes of just three years before. While there were a few pessimistic forecasters arguing that a crash was coming, most people had no idea anything was wrong with the financial system.

From those peaks in July and September 2005, the collapse began. By mid-2007, new single-family home sales were down 44 percent, and existing home sales were down 21 percent. In other words, the

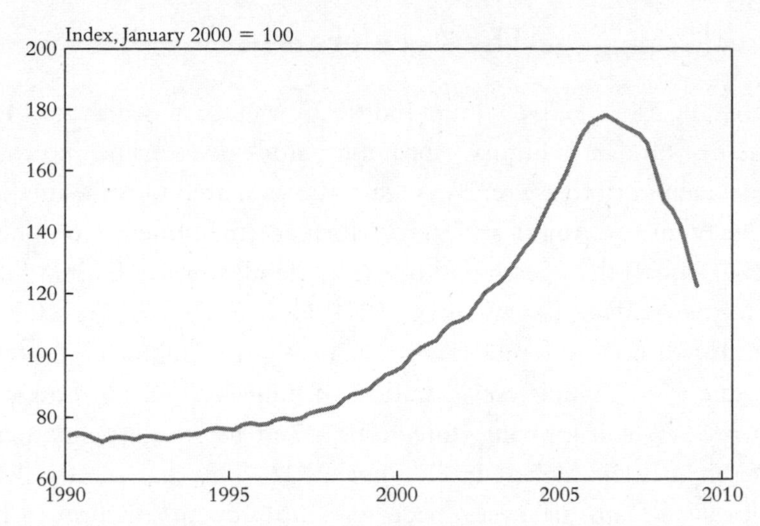

Figure 4.3 Case-Shiller Home Price Index, 20-City Average
SOURCE: S&P/Case-Shiller

housing market was well into crisis before August 2007. Housing had been collapsing for at least two years before the subprime crisis became a household word.

Construction activity continued to rise for many months after sales peaked, with housing starts reaching the astounding level of 2.273 million units at an annual rate in January 2007. This was roughly 40 percent higher than the lowest level of 2003, and nearly 700,000 more starts than population growth and teardowns require. This led to a surge in inventory. It was only a matter of time before prices fell. In July 2006, the Case Schiller 20-city home price index peaked at more than double the index level of 2000. By August 2007, prices were down 4.5 percent, and then fell another 16.5 percent in the next 12 months, the worst decline in home prices since at least the Great Depression. (See Figure 4.3.)

Put all of this together and it is clear that housing sales, housing construction, and housing prices all peaked before the panic actually began. In fact, housing sales were falling at rates that were typical of previous recessions almost a full year before the markets ever sensed there was a serious problem brewing.

The Acceleration

On July 19, 2007, the Dow Jones Industrial Average closed above 14,000 for the first time in its history. Apparently, stock investors had no clue of what was about to transpire. By August, things started to come unglued.

On August 6, American Home Mortgage Investment Corporation (AHMI), the 10th largest retail mortgage lender in the United States, filed for bankruptcy. On August 9, BNP Paribas, a major French bank, suspended three investment funds that invested in subprime mortgage debt, due to a "complete evaporation of liquidity."[3] Even though the economy was still growing, foreclosures and mortgage delinquencies had risen to their highest levels since 2002. This was mostly driven by mortgage loans that were made with little documentation to people with low or no incomes—so-called subprime mortgages. As these loans stopped performing, the market for subprime debt dried up.

At the peak, there was roughly $1.5 trillion in subprime debt outstanding, and a great deal of this had been securitized—packaged together. This required a number of steps. First, a mortgage lender would make a loan. Then that loan would be sold to a company that packaged these mortgages into investment pools. These pools, called mortgage-backed securities (MBSs) sometimes contained thousands of individual loans. Then these MBSs were sold to investors as a single bond.

As long as a market for these securities existed, the lending process would continue. Mostly, these securities were sold to hedge funds, or to special investment vehicles (SIVs) that were attached to larger banks. These funds used leverage (borrowing) to hold securities backed by mortgages or other assets (such as car loans or credit cards). Since they could borrow at very low short-term rates and leverage, they were willing to hold these securities at relatively low yields.

Looking back, rumblings of nervousness about these investments can be seen as early as 2006. Buyers of subprime MBSs started to slow purchases or even stop in 2006 and early 2007. Many firms that manufactured subprime securities, like Merrill Lynch, were still putting them together, but then were unable to sell them. As a result, they ended up holding tens of billions of dollars of their own inventory as liquidity dried up and the market collapsed.

It was these securities that were at the heart of the crisis from the beginning. Funds that bought them, manufacturers of the securities that got stuck holding them, and the originators of the loans all started taking on losses very rapidly as the markets turned illiquid and prices fell to rock-bottom, fire-sale levels.

Why in the World Were They Doing That?

Before we get to the financial collapse that all this caused, it is important to understand why so many people were involved in this seemingly inane process of lending money to people who could not repay.

The first thing to realize is that the whole idea of creating more homeowners has been a goal of government (really of Americans) for a very long time. President Bush said in 2002, "You see, we want everybody in America to own their own home. That's what we want." President Bush also came up with the idea of a "homeownership gap."

> Two-thirds of all Americans own their homes, yet we have a problem here in America because fewer than half of the Hispanics and half the African Americans own a home. That's a homeownership gap. It's a—it's a gap that we've got to work together to close for the good of our country, for the sake of a more hopeful future. We've got to work to knock down the barriers that have created a homeownership gap.[4]

On December 13, 2003, President Bush signed into law the American Dream Down Payment Act, a $200 million fund to help low-income Americans buy homes. This was just the latest in a long list of laws and rules designed to help people buy and own homes. Our tax rules, which allow the deduction of mortgage interest, are just one piece of evidence. There are many others, but all we really need to know is that just about everyone, Democrats and Republicans, left and right, thought owning a home was nothing but good. It was the American Dream.

Government has always looked for ways to increase homeownership. In addition, better technology made it easier to apply for and deliver credit. The late Edward Gramlich, former governor of the Federal Reserve and professor of economics at the University of Michigan, laid the reasons out in an August 31, 2007, speech in Jackson Hole, Wyoming.[5] He said there were "many causes" for the "boom" in housing. They included a 1980 change in usury laws, so that "it was no longer illegal for lenders to make higher-priced mortgages." After the change, banks could charge higher interest rates if a borrower's credit was not strong. He added that "automatic underwriting played a role, as did securitization, which enabled lenders to spread risk more efficiently."

But then he also added that the Community Reinvestment Act (CRA) "gave banks an incentive to make low—and moderate—income mortgages." This was a classic Gramlich understatement. What he describes as an "incentive" was actually a potential penalty. The CRA forced banks to do business in "every" area that they might possibly be collecting deposits. So a bank in Chicago needed to do some business on the West Side, where poverty is rampant, or face penalties.

Clinton-era changes to the CRA laws put more teeth in them, requiring banks to use "innovative and flexible" lending practices in addressing the needs of low-income neighborhoods.[6] As Larry Lindsey, former Federal Reserve Board governor and head of the Fed committee that handled CRA wrote, "It was never the financial services industry (in my experience) that lobbied for easier lending terms. Rather it was politicians who sought easier lending regulations so more constituents could borrow."[7]

In this same vein, Fannie Mae and Freddie Mac were also used by government to keep mortgage rates low. Because Fannie and Freddie had the implicit backing of the federal government, they could borrow at very low cost in the credit markets. Fannie and Freddie are also exempt from all state and local taxes. These two benefits allowed Fannie and Freddie to operate at much lower cost than their private-sector competitors.

By the mid-2000s, Fannie and Freddie had taken over more than 50 percent of the conventional mortgage market and became the single most important source of liquidity in this arena. Because of their government-subsidized advantage, they outcompeted the private sector.

This forced many private banks to move out the risk curve—into the realm of subprime and Alt-A mortgages for people with either lower credit ratings or a desire to limit paperwork. This was the only place that private-sector firms could compete. Then in 2005, Fannie and Freddie moved into the subprime marketplace in a big way, driving down rates, reducing spreads, and causing the market to become even bigger and make even riskier loans.

At the same time, ratings agencies, which are approved by Congress and therefore have limited competition, were consistently rating subprime mortgage pools double- or triple-A. The end result of all of this was that the mortgage market itself was distorted by government rules, regulations, and institutions. These distortions created an unstable market that would have collapsed eventually, even without the Federal Reserve's lowering the federal funds rate to 1 percent in 2003 and encouraging even more lending and leverage.

The idea that greedy bankers, unprodded by government incentives, were just writing mortgages, packaging mortgages, selling mortgages, and encouraging others to do the same all for the commissions and bonuses has never been true. The government encouraged this market to develop and hardly ever seemed to worry about it. As long as interest rates were low and banks could securitize assets into triple-A-rated pools, investors were willing to buy them. This finally changed when the Fed lifted rates enough to bring it to a stop.

Before that, in April 2005, when he was still chairman of the Fed, Alan Greenspan gave a speech at the Fed's Community Affairs Conference. In that speech, he practically waved the pom-poms in the air for subprime loans.

> Where once more marginal applicants would simply have been denied credit, lenders are now able to quite efficiently judge the risk posed by individual applicants and to price that risk appropriately. These improvements have led to rapid growth in subprime mortgage lending; indeed, today subprime mortgages account for roughly 10 percent of the number of all mortgages outstanding, up from just 1 or 2 percent in the early 1990s.[8]

So Why Blame Capitalists?

Despite all this evidence, the popular press just will not support the idea that government was a huge part of the problems we are facing today. In fact, some in the press actively defend the government because they do not want to be cut off from scoops.

Steve Liesman, a journalist who reports on economics for CNBC, was confronted on air about this issue back on June 17, 2009 by Rick Santelli, a former trader who also reports for CNBC from the floor of the Chicago Board of Trade. Rick said that he blamed "mostly government" for our financial problems. Liesman angrily responded, "You have yet to show me the government order that forced the banks to make stupid loans. . . . Where's the government order that said regardless of what the leverage ratios are . . . where's the one that said 'sign this stupid loan?' Where's the one that said 'you must sign this stupid loan?' You must lend to people who can't [repay]. You must securitize."[9]

Liesman's position is extreme, and it's wrong. The CRA forced banks to lend in neighborhoods that would face much higher odds of financial difficultly, and it forced them to use "innovative" practices to do so. If banks did not lend, they faced potential problems from their regulators or from community organizers.

Fannie Mae and Freddie Mac also distorted the market with help from the government, and every ratings agency (which gave those triple-A ratings) must be approved by Congress before it can rate any bonds. Finally, the argument that government did not "force" Wall Street to do what it did turns a blind eye to the biggest issue—the Fed.

With Alan Greenspan at the helm, the Fed pushed the federal funds rate down to 1 percent, creating a mirage of cheap and easy money for investors and borrowers alike. Everyone thought they were making wise decisions when, in reality, the Fed was fooling them. Money was not supposed to be that cheap, and it couldn't stay that cheap for long. When combined with technological developments that made mortgage lending easier, these government mistakes created frenzied activity in the housing market that was destined to end badly.

The housing market collapse that led to the Panic of 2008 was certainly caused by government. This does not mean that Wall Street did not have a role. The buyers of homes and the banks that leveraged up to lend to them should have been more circumspect about excessively low interest rates and continuously rising house prices. As they say, "something that is too good to be true probably is too good to be true."

When government is encouraging a housing boom in every way it can, that's exactly what will happen. To ignore this and then turn around and blame the private sector for the boom is either denial or purposeful obfuscation. But since government controls the bully pulpit and history is written by the victors, the private sector takes the blame. That's too bad, because it's just not true.

Chapter 5

Who Makes Your Glasses?

A major impediment to understanding the economy is that most people think about it from a modern vantage point. We have erected institutions and entities that cloud the picture. Many things that used to occur naturally have been institutionalized. This is not always bad, but it sure can cause confusion.

For example, many people think that the Federal Reserve controls interest rates. And there is also a widespread belief that the Treasury Department can move the value of the dollar at will, or oil companies can control oil prices, or China can do just about anything it wants.

All of these examples have a seed of truth. Every market participant, especially those with government power, can influence markets. But the power that many ascribe to these entities is vastly overstated. The Fed does have total control over the federal funds rate—the overnight interest rate that banks charge for lending to or borrowing from each other—and through this rate influences all short-term interest rates. But that does not mean the Fed actually controls interest rates. They certainly don't control long-term interest rates.

But that's not the major point. The major point is more fundamental. Human action determines interest rates. They are a naturally occurring phenomenon. They would exist whether or not the Fed, or banks, or the Treasury Department, or business news, or any other entity existed. So when the Fed sets short-term interest rates, those rates may or may not be equal to the true, underlying rate of interest. Just because the Fed has settled on an interest rate does not mean it is the "right" rate.

There are two different interest rates in the world. There is one rate that would exist without any government interference—and this is called the "natural rate." And there is another rate that the government (mainly the Fed) sets. These are not always equal. And when they are not equal, when the Fed puts rates above or below the natural rate, bad things can happen.

In fact, the key reason for the financial crisis of recent years is that the Fed set interest rates too low. This encouraged excessive borrowing, leverage, and risk-taking. Low interest rates created a "mirage" that many market participants could not see through. Low interest rates from the Fed caused borrowers and lenders to put on a pair of glasses that provided a deceptive view. And many market participants made decisions that in retrospect look foolish.

Are Consumers Rational?

Many analysts disagree with this and argue that the financial crisis was caused by a greed-induced credit binge. According to this view, not only did banks extend too much credit and perpetrate deception on borrowers, but consumers and other investors went overboard and became overleveraged. They just borrowed too much.

New York Times columnist David Brooks, whom many people consider conservative, subscribes to this view. He argues that the old ideas of classical economics—that people behave rationally—just don't work anymore.

"This view [classical economics] explains a lot," he wrote, "but not the current financial crisis—how so many people could be so stupid, incompetent and self-destructive all at once. The crisis has delivered a blow to classical economics. . . . "[1] Brooks's view of the world today is that "[w]e have moved from The Age of Leverage to The Great Unwinding."[2] He and others think that we have lived through a "bubble," an unstable and irrational "binge" of borrowing.

Brooks probably doesn't even realize it, but this is a demand-side argument. It is a total sellout to John Maynard Keynes, who believed "animal spirits" drove consumer behavior. Keynes argued that people are driven by emotion. Here is the key passage on this issue from *The General Theory of Employment, Interest and Money*, his most famous book:

> Even apart from the instability due to speculation, there is the instability due to the characteristic of human nature that a large proportion of our positive activities depend on spontaneous optimism rather than mathematical expectations, whether moral or hedonistic or economic. Most, probably, of our decisions to do something positive, the full consequences of which will be drawn out over many days to come, can only be taken as the result of animal spirits—a spontaneous urge to action rather than inaction, and not as the outcome of a weighted average of quantitative benefits multiplied by quantitative probabilities.[3]

A widespread consensus seems to be that Keynes was prescient about the Panic of 2008. It was greed and envy—"animal spirits"—not rational behavior that caused people to buy too many houses and borrow too much money. But this is a very narrow view of the problem.

If we can prove that the Fed manipulated interest rates, then the decisions people made might not have been irrational at all. Expectations about what is true and false matter greatly when we analyze behavior. For example, when you come to a green light in your car, you keep going because you assume that the light from the cross street is red. You don't stop, park your car, and walk around to the other side and check. You trust that the other light is red and you rationally keep going. Rational behavior often depends on assumptions.

If the Fed sets the overnight rate at 1 percent, and banks trust the Fed, they will behave as if 1 percent is the "right" interest rate. And when the bank is then willing to market 2 percent teaser mortgages, a borrower will also *assume* that this interest rate is the "right" one.

Banks and borrowers will "trust" this rate and make decisions based on it, particularly when the Fed had not set rates at artificially low levels for many years. Like the green traffic light, why should anyone go around to the other side, or go back to school to get an economics degree in order to prove that what they see is real and true. After all, wasn't Alan Greenspan considered the "maestro"? Wasn't he considered omnipotent—the smartest guy in any room?

This creates a serious problem. If the Fed pushes interest rates below the "natural rate" and people believe that the Fed's rate is the right rate, many will view debt as less risky, or at least less costly, than they would if interest rates were higher. These people are not being irrational or greedy, and none of this has anything to do with animal spirits.

People were being rational, not stupid. People are not animals. In fact, a belief that animal spirits drive consumer decisions smacks of some serious intellectual arrogance, which is certainly not conservative. It also completely ignores the fact that the Fed can deceive the entire world about the true cost of money.

What Is the Natural Rate of Interest?

This entire thought process is driven by the idea that interest rates are a natural phenomenon. It revolves around the idea that people, without the need for any government entity, think about the time value of their resources as they make decisions on a daily basis. To understand this, a thought experiment can help.

So let's close our eyes. Well, you can't do that and still read, so just imagine that your local neighborhood has been transported back in time a few hundred years. Imagine that you and your neighbors are self-sufficient farmers and ranchers. You grow your own food and raise your own animals for slaughter. Every spring, summer, and fall you grow and then store underground your vegetables and grains, and you slaughter and smoke, dry, or salt your meat. You do this so that you can survive during the winter. You live in an era of subsistence living. There are no savings per se, except for what you need during the winter, but come spring even this is gone, and you start all over again.

In this world there is no need for interest rates, banks, or any of the institutions or tools that we take for granted these days. Because savings do not really exist, there are very few assets and no debt. It may sound peaceful, but life hangs by a thread all the time. If a drought comes, or your animals get sick, you can starve to death. There is no refrigeration, and storage facilities are minimal, so storing up excess (if it ever exists) is virtually impossible.

Imagine that you became very adept at this process. You are blessed with an ability to get more from your land than your neighbors, so much so that you can grow and raise enough for two families. You also notice that one of your neighbors just can't get it right; they barely make it through the winter. But even though your neighbor can barely scratch out a living on the land, he sure is a good carpenter. He can build just about anything.

I think you can tell where this is going. When there is surplus, there is opportunity. As Say's Law tells us, "supply creates its own demand."[4] It is the extra food that creates the demand for the barn. So you come up with a proposal: You will feed your neighbor and his family (out of your surplus) for the next two years if he builds you a barn.

It's a simple transaction. But, if you think about it, it requires some complex analysis. There is a risk that one or both of you may not be able to fulfill your end of the bargain. Weather, sickness, and injury could all disrupt the agreed-upon trade. Materials could become scarce. Tools could break. Anything could happen. Moreover, it takes place over time, and when there is a transfer of consumption over time an interest rate is implied. There is a time value of resources, what we call the "time value of money" these days. But remember, in our imaginary world there is no money.

If you could trade for a fully completed barn right now, you would give less food for it than would be necessary over a two-year period. Risk is one reason. But time is the main reason. Transactions that take place over time by their very nature are risky and have opportunity cost. As we have already noted, many things could go wrong. But it is also true that you are now deciding to live here for two more years, which means you cannot move or spend your time on anything else. This is opportunity cost.

One way to measure this cost—this time value of resources—is by determining the interest rate. And, in this case, the interest rate is equal to the difference between the food that the builder of the barn would demand for an already completed barn today, versus the amount that would be required over a two-year period.

We go through all of this to show that interest rates are a natural phenomenon. We don't need money, the Fed, banks, business television, futures markets, or the Treasury Department. All we need is two people who want to make a deal. The interest rate just "drops out" of the transaction. Because people exist and because they interact, interest rates exist.

Ludwig von Mises and other Austrian economists[5] theorized the existence of a natural rate, sometimes called the "neutral" rate of interest. This rate would "always coincide with the ratio between the prices of present goods and the prices of future goods, under the assumption that all prices change uniformly."[6] At a "neutral rate of interest" a consumer would be indifferent between present and future goods.

But the Fed can control a key short-term interest rate, and it sets that rate based on a host of factors that may or may not have anything to do with the natural rate. And if the Fed sets that rate too low, then the process of economic decision making will be disrupted and people will value present goods more than future goods. When savings earn a low rate of interest, why save? And when debt is inexpensive, why not borrow?

Calculating the Natural Rate

This idea of a natural rate of interest (or neutral rate) can be extrapolated to our current world relatively easily. The only difference is that today we have millions or billions of potential goods and services and people to think about. Every activity, and every investment, has price, risk, and return associated with it.

Consumers and investors have an endless set of decisions to make when it comes to their resources (purchasing, saving, and investing). These decisions are based on needs, wants, desires, age, risk tolerance, and a host of other issues. But this doesn't make things that much more complicated. There is still an interest rate that balances all of this—a natural rate that will "fall out" of all these desires and decisions.

We don't need the Fed to tell us what it is. We don't need a government entity to put ceilings or floors on interest rates or to regulate how much people borrow or lend. In fact, all those potential interferences with the market can only mess things up. If interest rates were allowed to move naturally with the rate of growth of the economy and the true supply and demand for credit, most people would make much better decisions.

Calculating the natural rate is not really that difficult. If we think about it, this rate should balance credit availability across all potential decisions. So, a good proxy for interest rates would be the overall growth rate of the economy—what economists call nominal gross domestic product (GDP). Nominal GDP includes both inflation and real growth, and, as we know, interest rates should incorporate both of these factors.

Nominal GDP measures the "average" rate of growth of all businesses. Some businesses, like Google, have been growing much faster than GDP. Other businesses, like the *New York Times*, have actually been contracting. The average of all these growth rates—the companies and sectors growing faster, those growing the same, and those growing slower—is equal to the growth rate of nominal GDP.

If interest rates were equal to nominal GDP, then only projects that promised returns above the average growth rate of the economy would be funded. If interest rates are set at a level that is less than GDP growth, then some will decide to invest in below-average projects because they look profitable. If interest rates are held well above GDP, then only very profitable (well above average) projects would be funded, and some projects that promised higher than GDP returns (but were still below the set interest rate) would not get funded.

All of the preceding is based on the fact people will borrow and invest if they think a spread—an arbitrage profit—exists. If money costs 3 percent, but the project returns 6 percent, then a spread of 3 percent is apparently available. Only projects that have returns that exceed the cost of borrowing should attract resources and capital. If interest rates are 6 percent, but the project returns only 3 percent, then there would be a negative arbitrage—a loss of 3 percent per year on this investment—and it would not be funded.

The Nominal GDP Rule

The preceding analysis explains how I came to believe that the rate of change in nominal GDP is the best measure of the natural, or neutral, rate of interest. And the statistical evidence suggested that it was best to smooth the growth rate over eight quarters, or two years. A one-year growth rate is just too volatile.

This made sense because the natural rate is not likely to jump up and down in dramatic fashion. As a result, the eight-quarter annualized growth rate of nominal GDP (total spending) reflects a smoothed average rate of overall economic growth. This, it turns out, is a pretty darn good estimate of the natural rate of interest.

The real proof of the model can be found in its performance. In Figure 5.1, the dark line represents the annualized eight-quarter average growth rate of nominal GDP for the United States. The light gray line is the actual federal funds rate as determined by the Federal Reserve.

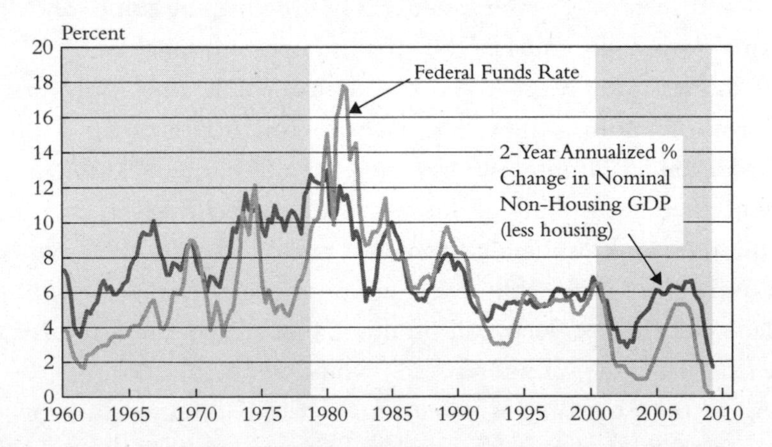

Figure 5.1 Eight-Quarter Nominal GDP versus Federal Funds Rate
SOURCE: Federal Reserve Board, BLS

For the sake of our analysis, I have divided this chart into three periods. The two shaded areas—between 1960 and 1979 and between 2001 and 2009—are periods of time when the Fed held the federal funds rate mostly below nominal GDP growth. The period from 1979 to 2000 is a 20-year period when the Fed mostly held interest rates close to or above nominal GDP growth.

After 16 years of using this approach to gauge monetary policy, it has become apparent that there are special periods of time where one sector of the economy or another forces an adjustment. For example, in the late 1990s, especially during the run-up to Y2K, technology spending was adding significantly to GDP growth. During the year ending in September 1999, nominal GDP without technology grew one-half percent slower than total nominal GDP (which included the turbocharged tech sector).

The natural rate of interest was higher for technology companies than it was for the rest of the economy, particularly manufacturing. Therefore, as the Fed lifted interest rates in 1999 and 2000, the impact on the nontech economy was dramatic. What appeared to be a small rate increase relative to the economy as a whole was actually a large rate hike for the nontech economy, which was growing more slowly.

The end result was that the rate hikes of 1999–2000, when Alan Greenspan lifted the federal funds rates from 4.75 percent to 6.5 percent, were actually too much for the economy to take. Not only did a recession occur, but deflationary pressures appeared for the first time in 50 years. And, as it turns out, this was the monetary policy mistake that led the Fed to overcorrect and lower interest rates too much in 2001–2004.

In the past four or five years, it has been the housing sector that has been more volatile than the economy. At first, it added significantly to GDP; lately, it has been subtracting from GDP. For example, during the eight quarters ending in the second quarter of 2009, overall nominal GDP has averaged just 0.5 percent growth, which means the natural rate is close to one-half of one percent. But, nonhousing, nominal GDP has averaged 1.7 percent during the same period of time.

With the Fed holding the funds rate between 0 percent and 0.25 percent, it would appear that monetary policy is either slightly easy (if we compare to overall nominal GDP) or very easy (if we compare to nonhousing nominal GDP). Either way, the economy is set for Fed-induced rebound. And when it rebounds, the natural rate will rise. The longer it takes the Fed to hike rates as that happens, the easier monetary policy will become.

Money and the Interest Rates

But before we get bogged down in recent history, we must understand how monetary theory enters the picture. The Fed controls the level of the federal funds rate by adding or subtracting reserves to/from the banking system. The Fed buys bonds from banks to inject money into the system and sells bonds to banks to subtract money from the system.

If the Fed wants to drive the federal funds rates below the natural rate, it buys bonds and injects reserves. If it wants to drive interest rates up, it subtracts reserves. Like any market, an increase in supply will drive down the price, while a decrease in supply will drive up the price. And in this case, the supply is money and the "price" is the interest rate.

The end result of all this analysis is that we can tell when the Fed is adding excess liquidity to the system and when it is subtracting liquidity. We do this by watching the level of the actual funds rate compared to our estimate of the natural rate.

The actual interest rate was well below the natural rate prior to 1979 and then again after 2001, signaling easy money. But the rate was close to or above the natural rate for most of the period between 1979 and 2000, signaling a tight or neutral monetary policy. Commodity prices increased in the 1970s, collapsed and then settled into a range during the 1980s and 1990s, and then moved sharply higher in the past eight years. In other words, commodity prices are a convincing sign that the model works. And with the federal funds rate below the natural rate right now, inflationary pressures will be on the rise in the years ahead.

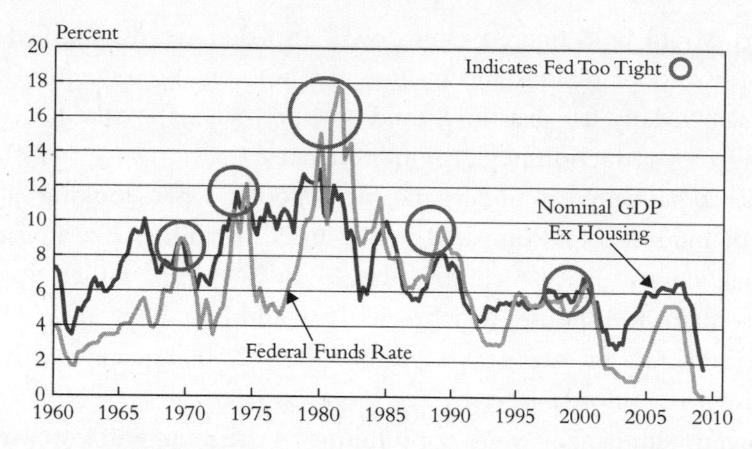

Figure 5.2 Recessions Follow Fed Rate Hikes
SOURCE: Federal Reserve Board, BLS

In addition, the model is a solid indicator of an excessively tight, or recessionary, Fed policy. When the Fed tightened, as can be seen in the circles in Figure 5.2, the subtraction of liquidity caused recessions in 1969–1970, 1972–1974, 1979–1982, 1989–1990, and 1999–2000.

The Fed-Induced Bubble

This model proves that monetary policy mistakes were at the heart of the recent financial crisis. Not only did the Fed overtighten in 1999–2000; it caused excessive credit creation in housing during the early 2000s. The Fed cut the federal funds rate dramatically in 2001, from a level that was above the natural rate to a level that was well below the natural rate.

At that time, the Fed and others provided a very long list of reasons that interest rates should be as low as they were. They argued that deflation was the real threat, not inflation. Many argued that China and India and other large, well-populated countries would continue to drive down wage rates and inflationary pressures.

Ben Bernanke, then a governor on the Federal Reserve Board, argued that a "global savings glut"[7] had emerged. Because consumers in China and other Asian countries were such huge savers, their savings would hold interest rates down. In other words, the Fed had a laundry list of reasons and excuses for holding interest rates down artificially. Many felt that this would be a permanent—or at least very long-term—reduction in global interest rates.

What happened is understandable. People, when looking at the level of interest rates compared to the prices of things like houses—especially house price increases—began to buy. And rather than an 1,800-square-foot house, which is what would have been affordable at the natural rate of interest, people bought a 2,500-square-foot house because it was affordable at the Fed's interest rates.

Investment bankers were not immune to the mirage of lower interest rates either. They, just like almost everyone, were convinced that very low interest rates were a permanent fixture. To blame people for greed, gluttony, and stupidity when the Fed was providing them with an artificial input to the decision making process is just not fair.

Without the Fed's holding interest rates artificially low, there is no way that the financial market problems of recent years would have ever occurred. The sad part is that in order to protect itself, the Federal Reserve blames the consumer, banks, investment banks, and anyone else who fell prey to its deception. Capitalism is taking the brunt of the blame, when in fact it was government that caused the mirage.

Wall Street should have known better, and it deserves part of the blame. After all, there were many people warning about excessively low interest rates, including the *Wall Street Journal* editorial page. But an overwhelming part of the blame can be heaped on the Federal Reserve, and Alan Greenspan in particular, for holding interest rates below the natural rate.

Greenspan has attempted to defend himself in many ways, like writing op-eds and giving speeches, but perhaps his most desperate move was in testimony to the U.S. House Committee on Oversight and Government Reform. He threw the private sector and his supposed belief in capitalism under the bus when he told the Committee: "Those of us who have looked to the self-interest of lending institutions to protect shareholders' equity, myself included, are in a state of shocked disbelief."

In other words, he blames the banks and the people behind them for the crisis, not himself. He is basically arguing that free-market capitalism doesn't work and that people are not rationally self-interested. It's almost as if he is saying people should not have believed the Fed. They should have thought three times before believing that 1 percent interest rates were correct. They should never have assumed that going through a green light was actually safe.

We've Been Here Before

It's not like this hasn't happened before. In the 1960s and 1970s, for almost 20 consecutive years, the Fed was too easy. It held the federal funds rate below the natural rate for a very long time. This meant that the Fed was printing excess money—adding too much liquidity to the system—for a considerable period.

The results were not surprising. Consumer price inflation averaged just 1.2 percent per year in the five years between 1958 and 1963. It then accelerated sharply. Between 1963 and 1968, the consumer price index increased 2.8 percent per year; it increased 5.4 percent a year from 1968 to 1973, and then 8.0 percent per year between 1973 and 1978. The five-year inflation rate peaked at 10 percent during the five years ending in 1981, with annual inflation of 14 percent in early 1980.

This inflation was not that difficult to forecast. In order for the Fed to hold interest rates below the natural rate, it was forced to add excess liquidity to the market. But inflation was only part of the problem. As they did between 2001 and 2007, low interest rates encouraged overinvestment. But back then, in the 1970s, it was agriculture and energy markets that really got overheated. Housing boomed, too, but nothing like the 2000s because government was trying to boost other areas of the economy back then.

In the 1970s, Department of Agriculture Secretary Earl Butz encouraged farmers to plant "fencerow to fencerow," while he subsidized exports to the Soviet Union. Farm price supports and the Farm Credit System, combined with already low interest rates, encouraged farmers to buy more land and grow more crops. Acreage devoted to corn and wheat production soared; crop prices doubled in the early 1970s and then remained high, while farmland prices increased by 400 percent. With the Fed holding interest rates well below their natural rate, borrowing to expand a farm was a no-brainer. Farm debt increased 236 percent between 1971 and 1981, while nominal gross domestic product (GDP) expanded just 177 percent.

The same thing was happening in the oil patch. A little-known bank headquartered in a strip mall in Oklahoma City started making oil loans. Eventually, Penn Square Bank became ground zero for the oil bust, just like Countrywide Financial and IndyMac were key players in the subprime mortgage crisis.

In the 1970s, everyone (including President Jimmy Carter) thought the world was running out of oil. Oil prices climbed from $2.92 per barrel in 1965 to $11.16 per barrel in 1975 to $39.50 per barrel in 1980. For most people, this increase in prices was "proof" that oil was in short supply. With oil prices and agricultural prices rising, there were certain parts of the world—like Latin America—that looked very attractive. They produced food *and* energy. So banks that were awash in deposits from OPEC countries began to recycle those petro-dollars to Latin America.

Of course, all of this was a mirage. Easy money in the 1970s (measured by the fact that the federal funds rate was well below nominal GDP growth) was creating inflation. And with rates held artificially low, lending in areas that were growing faster than the economy seemed like good business.

You can still hear the echoes of time gone by. "God ain't making any more farmland," the farmers and the farmers' bankers would tell themselves. "Peak oil is here and prices will never come down again," the oilmen and the oilmen's bankers would say.

If this doesn't sound familiar, then you weren't paying attention. In the 2000s, the entire boom in housing and home lending was based on a belief that house prices would never fall. Housing prices, according to the Case-Shiller 20-city average, had climbed 8.5 percent per year for 10 years between 1995 and 2005. No wonder lending exploded. Interest rates were not only well below the natural rate, but they were well below the annual increase in home prices. It was an arbitrage made in heaven.

Stupid Bankers, or Not?

In retrospect, the 1970s lending boom in agriculture, oil and Latin America, was a mistake, just like the lending of the 2000s on housing was a mistake. But the deception was not being perpetrated by Wall Street. It was the Fed and the government that were doing the deceiving. Farmers, oilmen, banks, home buyers, and hedge funds were the ones that looked at interest rates, believed they represented reality, and behaved accordingly. People bought into the idea that interest rates were permanently low and that prices for agriculture products, oil, and housing would continue to rise.

This explains everything. Even lending 10 percent more than a house was worth to someone who might not be able to repay was not really a big risk. Housing prices would continue to move up, and the cost of money was very, very low. So all a lender had to do was take over the property, and since it was still rising in price, the value of the property would eventually make up for any losses from the loan.

Leverage was looked at in the same vein. Hedge funds and other leveraged investment vehicles could borrow at very low short-term interest rates and earn the spread between those borrowing costs and what they could earn by lending for houses, cars, or credit cards. The competition for consumer loans became so intense that spreads declined to very low levels. And as those spreads declined, leverage increased. Leveraging 20:1 when spreads were 2 percent earned the investor 40 percent. But when spreads fell to just 1 percent, they were forced to leverage 40:1 to earn the same return. Again, this was not considered risky because interest rates would remain low—even the Fed said this—and because house prices would continue to rise.

Most of the increase in consumer borrowing during the 2000s was for mortgages. Mortgage loans, including second mortgages and lines of credit, grew by 134 percent between 2000 and 2007, from $4.5 trillion to $10.5 trillion. Consumer credit, which includes auto loans and credit cards, grew by just 64 percent. This makes sense. Because loans tied to housing were backed up by collateral that was rising in value.

The bankers knew exactly what they were doing. Unfortunately, what they were doing was a mistake. Just like the 1970s, artificially low interest rates had created an environment that was deceptive. It was a mirage. The glasses that people were looking through were made by the Fed, and those glasses provided a warped sense of reality.

It Always Ends Badly: Volcker to the Rescue

Ludwig von Mises called the investment, or at least much of the investment, that occurs during periods of time when the monetary authorities hold interest rates artificially low, "mal-investment"—bad investment. When interest rates are below the average growth rate of the economy, many projects that are not really good projects get funded.

And, because returns for all investments appear better than they really are, overinvestment in an area that is doing well sets the market up for a fall. Low interest rates led to an oversupply of housing and eventually declining prices. When that happens, defaults and bankruptcies rise. One of two things brings the boom to an end—either the Fed lifts rates and changes the dynamics of the process or the weight of the overinvestment finally pulls the whole system down.

For the lending of the 1970s, it was the former. In the fourth quarter of 1979, Paul Volcker lifted the federal funds rate above 13 percent, which was above the two-year change in nominal GDP. After more than five consecutive years, the funds rate was finally above the natural rate. And then, for four more years, monetary policy (as measured by the nominal GDP rule) was tight.

Commodity prices, including grains and energy products, collapsed, while farmland rolled over and headed down. Loans to farmers and to oil producers started to go bad, and Latin American economies faltered. On top of this, the economy fell into one of the most severe recessions since the Great Depression.

Penn Square Bank collapsed in July 1982 as its oil loans went bad. And as this happened, other banks took losses, too. Penn Square had been selling "oil loan participations." These participations were not as sophisticated as the mortgage-backed securities of the past decade, but the idea was exactly the same. Loans were sliced up into smaller pieces and sold to other banks. Banks that had participated in these loans, such as Continental Illinois Bank and Trust Company of Chicago (the nation's seventh-largest bank) and Seafirst Bank of Seattle, were dragged down as well.

Seafirst Bank was taken over by Bank of America in 1983, just before it was declared insolvent. Continental was declared insolvent in May 1984, after it was forced to write down more than $500 million of Penn Square loans and large depositors withdrew $10 billion. The government took over Continental because it was considered too big to fail.

Between 1980 and 1995, nearly 2,800—yes, nearly 2,800—banks and savings and loan companies (S&Ls) failed or required government assistance. In addition, every Latin American country defaulted on its debts, and every money center bank in the United States was basically insolvent. Not since the Great Depression had the United States experienced such a serious banking crisis.

The S&L debacle was also a direct result of the monetary mistakes of the 1970s. The largest asset on the books of S&Ls was mortgage loans. And during the 1970s inflationary boom in real estate prices, S&Ls made hundreds of billions of fixed-rate, long-term mortgage loans at interest rates that were well below the natural rate. This, as we have seen time and time again, is an accident waiting to happen.

As long as all interest rates were low, and the yield curve was upwardly sloping, there was no problem. S&Ls were paying depositors less than they were earning on their mortgage loans. But when Paul Volcker took over the Fed and jacked up short-term rates, the problems began. S&Ls were paying more to depositors than they were earning on their loans.

In this case, the lack of a securitization process was a huge negative. S&Ls could not get rid of their loans, even at a loss, without selling the whole institution. There was no market, as we know of it today, for individual mortgages. As a result, S&Ls experienced losses quarter after quarter because deposits cost them more than their assets earned.

Then . . .

When we add up all the potentially bad loans and losses experienced by financial institutions in the early 1980s, it appears that our problems were much worse then. The crisis that began in mid-2007 was much smaller.

If we assume a 30 percent loss rate on $1.5 trillion in subprime loans (a 60 percent default rate with only 50 percent recovery) and a 15 percent loss rate on Alt-A mortgage debt of about $1 trillion, the total "cost" of the initial mortgage crisis would have been $600 billion. This is just 0.4 percent of all assets in the U.S. economy and only about 4 percent of annual GDP.

In 1981, just the Latin American debt held by the eight largest American banks was roughly $54 billion, which represented 263 percent of capital for these banks.[8] Total developing country debt skyrocketed. The *Wall Street Journal* described the potential problem this way:

> It doesn't show on any maps, but there's a new mountain on the planet, a towering $500 billion of debt run up by the developing countries, nearly all of it within a decade . . . to some analysts the situation looks starkly ominous, threatening a chain reaction of country defaults, bank failures and general depression matching that of the 1930s.[9]

Farm debt in the United States was $186 billion in 1983, oil loans totaled at least $50 billion, and mortgage debt was roughly $1 trillion. With the unemployment rate rising to 10.8 percent, and farmers going bankrupt every day, the total potential losses in the early 1980s were far in excess of the problems the United States faced in the middle of 2007. My calculations put total potential loan losses in the early 1980s at 6 percent of GDP and nearly 1 percent of total assets.

It was dicey at first, but the Fed did not panic and Paul Volcker held tough, fighting inflation with high interest rates and tight money. Government spending rose in the early 1980s (as the recession boosted typical government programs for the poor and needy), but then government spending fell as a share of GDP after 1983. Tax rates were cut, and despite the fact that hundreds of banks would fail on an annual average for the next 12 years, the economy began to recover. The stock market boomed, with the Dow Jones Industrial Average rising from 812 in March 1982 to 6,436 in December 1996.

. . . And Now

In other words, the United States survived, even thrived, during a period of time when banking problems were even more severe, at least at the beginning of the crisis, than existed in the past few years. Can the same thing happen all over again? The answer is "of course." But will it happen? And here the answer is "we don't know yet." It's an open question.

Government has made many mistakes. Spending is on the rise, tax rates are widely expected to go up in the years ahead, and the Fed has reduced interest rates to near zero. All of this is the opposite of what the U.S. government did in the 1980s. In fact, it's what happened in the 1970s.

But this is where opportunity is created. With the Fed holding interest rates below the natural rate of interest, and monetary policy so accommodative, a near-term economic boom is on the way. Just like 1975–1976, easy money will boost economic activity and the stock market even though government policy mistakes hold the potential to slow growth in the future.

The key to understanding this is to realize that the underlying problems of the U.S. financial system, while severe, were never as large as they seemed. The real reason everything seemed to spin out of control so rapidly was mark-to-market accounting.

This accounting rule created havoc, and it caused many people to doubt free-market capitalism. This is a mistake. The problems we have lived through in the past few years were created by government policy mistakes, not some underlying weakness in the system. To doubt the system and put our heads in the sand is a recipe for mediocrity. The markets have already priced in a level of negativity that is unwarranted. This creates opportunity for those who can see the real underlying strength of the economy through the fog created by misguided government policies.

Chapter 6

Mark-to-Market Mayhem

History shows that the government has made some pretty big bloopers, but perhaps none have been larger than allowing the Financial Accounting Standards Board (FASB) to start enforcing a very strict mark-to-market accounting rule in late 2007. The FASB forced financial firms and auditors to use "exit" prices to value securities rather than the price at which a willing buyer and seller would trade. The result: Broker quotes began to outweigh models or cash flows—even though the brokers admitted the quotes were nonbinding. Within a year, the United States was in the middle of the worst pure financial panic in 100 years. Coincidence? Absolutely not.

Also known as "fair value accounting," the FASB rule forced banks to book losses that had not yet occurred even for securities that the banks were willing to hold. Then many of those losses were forced to run through the balance sheet, which reduced regulatory capital. This pushed banks into insolvency or capital violation, despite the fact that cash flow was still sound.

This process led to crisis. Potential investors in banks balked at investing as long as markets for so-called toxic assets were illiquid. A vicious cycle began, in which banks were forced to write down loan losses that had yet to occur. This threatened financial insolvency, which in turn threatened other institutions, creating even more uncertainty over potential insolvency. This undermined the economy and led to even lower prices for financial assets, which impaired capital, starting the cycle all over again.

Every government program put in place during the crisis was an attempt to work around mark-to-market accounting. The original $700 billion TARP proposal, put forward by Treasury Secretary Hank Paulson in September 2008, was designed to take "troubled assets" off the books and protect banks from further write-downs.

But that was only one program. The Treasury and the Fed put together an alphabet soup of programs—AMLF, CAP, CPFF, MMIFF, PDCF, PPIP, TAF, TALF, TLGP, and TSLF[1]—all designed to get markets "working" again. Despite all these programs, markets continued to slide into the abyss during 2008 and early 2009 because mark-to-market accounting rules had chased private capital away.

The government should have never let this happen. And once it did, the negative affects were seen so clearly in 2008 that it should have suspended the rule immediately. This would have allowed banks to hold those troubled assets without having illiquid markets threaten their regulatory capital. Time is a huge benefit when dealing with a financial crisis. But the government chose to enforce and support fair value accounting and not give banks any time.

Why the government refused to address this issue for more than a year is not a complete mystery. The government wants to be in control of every situation, and mark-to-market accounting put the banking system on the defensive. This gave the government an advantage in any public relations combat. It also gave the government leverage over these institutions in any private negotiations, which is exactly where the government likes to be. Government likes to think that the world cannot get along without it.

Government Failure versus Market Failure

A nice metaphor for this government narcissism can be found in Tom Robbins's 1976 book *Even Cowgirls Get the Blues*. Robbins makes an interesting observation about our brains: "that pound and a half of chicken-colored goo so highly regarded (by the brain itself) . . . which is attributed such intricate and mysterious powers (it is the self-same brain that does the attributing). . . ."[2]

He's right, of course. Most people consider the brain the most important organ of the body. But we rarely stop to think that it's the brain itself that tells us this. Isn't this metaphor appropriate for our bureaucracy? Government, or its appointed agents, will always tell us that the economy can't get along without the government.

A perfect example of this was provided in a speech by Larry Summers to the Council on Foreign Relations on June 12, 2009. Summers, the former Treasury secretary for President Clinton, is now a top economic staffer for President Obama. He said the following:

> In the last generation, prior to the current crisis, we saw the Latin American debt crisis, the 1987 stock market crash, the commercial real estate collapse and S&L debacle, the Mexican financial crisis, the Asian financial crisis, the LTCM liquidity crisis, the bursting of the NASDAQ bubble, and Enron. That is one major crisis every three years.
>
> In each case, the financial system did not perform its intended function as a bearer and distributor of risk, but instead proved to be a creator of risk. Problems emanating from the financial sector in each case profoundly disrupted the lives of hundreds of thousands or even tens of millions of people. . . . That is why President Obama has made financial regulatory reform a central legislative priority. . . . While many of the details are complex, the necessary fixes come from the application of common sense in

an area where complexity can blind sophisticated observers to the obvious.[3]

Isn't it interesting that Dr. Summers blames the "financial system" for the problems of the last generation? At the same time he claims government can provide the fix. Not once in this speech, nor at any time in memory, has he even remotely suggested that any existing government policy—unless it was some sort of lessening of regulation—had a role in creating any of these financial market road bumps. When the government comes in for blame, politicians will always argue that some previous administration did too little or that it gave too much leeway to the private sector. Often, deregulation and tax cuts are blamed.

This is a very convenient view of the world. And it has a serious problem. It's just plain wrong. It also leads to wrong conclusions and therefore wrong remedies. Where else would you expect problems to surface? In a society that uses money, every problem shows up in the financial system. When a farmer goes bankrupt, the lender (the bank) takes a loss, too. And if enough farmers go bankrupt, the system is threatened. Even government blames its problems on money—a lack of it, of course.

None of the crises that Summers mentions were fatal for the economy. While it is true that the government reacted to "fix" every one of these crises, it is not clear whether those reactions were necessary. More importantly, those very same government fixes created even more problems down the road.

For example, while you could blame the financial system for the 1987 stock market crash—a 22.6 percent one-day drop in the Dow—many have observed that it was really caused by government manipulation of the dollar exchange rate. But no matter what you believe, it was this crisis that earned Alan Greenspan his stripes as a central banker. On Tuesday, October 20, 1987, the day following the crash, Greenspan released a one-sentence statement at 8:41 A.M. eastern time, before the market opened, that said the Fed stood ready to "serve as a source of liquidity to support the economic and financial system." When the markets calmed down, many gave Greenspan credit. Conventional wisdom believed that the economy would fall into recession after the crash, and the Fed cut the federal funds rate from 7.25 percent to 6.5 percent by February 1988.

The economy never did fall into recession. Growth actually accelerated. So did inflation. As a result, Greenspan was forced to take the rate cuts back and then push rates up even more. Eventually, the funds rate rose to 9.8 percent in 1989. This was well above the natural rate of interest and this caused a recession in 1990–1991. In other words, the rate cuts after the crash eventually forced more rate hikes than would have been necessary otherwise. This then precipitated a recession.

The Mexican peso crisis of 1994 occurred because the central bank printed too many pesos. By printing too many pesos, as it had done many times before, the Mexican government was forcing an eventual devaluation of its currency. Many years after the crisis was over, a World Bank study found that it was wealthy Mexicans that moved billions of dollars of assets out of Mexico because they feared this devaluation. This capital flight accelerated the peso collapse, which would have occurred regardless. The Mexican authorities, and seemingly Larry Summers, then turn around and blame the private financial system, not the government policy. Convenient, eh?

Enron went bankrupt in late 2001, after the recession of 2001 was over and after the 9/11 terrorist attacks. The executives at Enron perpetrated fraud. To suggest that Enron was representative of the entire U.S. financial system is a huge stretch. Not as much of a stretch as trying to claim Bernie Madoff is representative of the financial system, but close. Moreover, it was the response by the government to Enron, especially the destruction of Arthur Andersen, and the increased support for mark-to-market accounting, that set the stage for the Panic of 2008.

The idea that the government is a calming influence while the private sector creates risk is very one-sided. And the fact that government officials, especially ones that are biased toward more liberal economic policy, support this point of view is not surprising. But this doesn't make it true. Government failure is much more of a problem than market failure.

Some Mark-to-Market Accounting History

What many people do not realize is that mark-to-market accounting was in place during the Great Depression. Milton Friedman blames it for causing a majority of bank failures in the 1930s. It was finally suspended in 1938 by a commission of experts put together at the direction of Franklin Roosevelt. Between 1938 and 2007, only trading firms used fair value accounting. Banks marked only some of their assets to market prices. Loans and many investments were held at historical cost unless there was a major change in their performance.

This puts the lie to those short-sellers and others who argue that mark-to-market accounting is the only transparent accounting method and that without it no one will trust the system. The suspension of the accounting rule in 1938 coincided with the end of the Depression. The U.S. economy did just fine between 1938 and 2007. During those 69 years, there were no panics or depressions.

But when the Financial Accounting Standards Board (FASB)—the rule-setting body for U.S. accounting standards—put a stringent fair value accounting rule (Rule 157) back into place in November 2007, all hell broke loose. This is not a coincidence. Fair value accounting is a disaster.

One of the interesting things about all of this is that Enron—what many point to as the major justification behind the FASB's move to fair value accounting rules—used mark-to-market accounting for its energy trading business.[4] As long as energy prices were rising, they were able to report large profits. In fact, unrealized trading gains (mark-to-market profits) accounted for more than one-half of Enron's earnings in 2000.[5] But when energy prices started to fall and competition drove down spreads, Enron resorted to the creation of off-balance sheet "special purpose entities" where it could park assets and avoid write-downs.

No matter what the rules are, a person or group of people intent on committing fraud will do so. Everyone knows the intent of the rules, and most people try to live by that intent. But sometimes it is the rules themselves that create problems, which is the case with mark-to-market accounting.

Apparently, the practice of marking assets to current prices was part of accounting from the very beginning. In the late 1800s and early 1900s, company bookkeepers had wide latitude, but often used "current value" or "appraised value" accounting. This was used for all assets, not just financial assets. Bookkeepers marked (adjusted the values of) just about everything, including factories, machines, investments, land, and so on. In good times, companies marked up the value of assets and made their books look much better. In bad times, the practice made things look worse, which created volatility.

A recent Securities and Exchange Commission (SEC) study of historical accounting precedents found that:

> In the aftermath of the Great Depression, there was a general move to more "conservative" accounting. . . . This move away from "current value" accounting and towards the use of historic cost accounting for long-lived assets was strongly supported by Robert E. Healy, the first Chief Accountant of the SEC.[6]

Healy joked that, " . . . you can capitalize in some states practically everything except the furnace ashes in the basement."[7]

This practice created problems and he knew it. The value of assets (even hard assets) varied from year to year. Accounting for these swings distorted company valuations and increased volatility in earnings and economic activity. This volatility was one of the key reasons for suspending mark-to-market accounting in the late 1930s.

Mark-to-Market Creates Volatility

Imagine you have built a farm from scratch over 35 years. You have built fences, barns, and irrigation systems. You have invested in tractors and other equipment, and your livestock have multiplied. This farm now has a total net worth of $10 million and revenue of $1 million per year, while generating profits of $500,000.

Now imagine that the market price of your land, equipment, and inventory declines by 10 percent in one year—a total balance sheet loss of $1 million. If you were forced to mark your assets to market and run the losses through your income statement, one full year of revenue would be wiped out and you would book a loss of $500,000. In essence, this is what fair value accounting does. It forces you to take changes in asset values—that mean nothing to you because you plan on farming for years to come—as if they were actual business losses this year.

While calculating the market value of your farm provides some useful information, its value today has little to do with its ability to produce income. In this example, the ongoing income from farming did not change even though the accounting rules said it was a disastrous year. The farm still produced $1 million in revenue and cash profits of $500,000. Of course, if asset values increased, the farm would write up these values and book higher profits and income.

And this is where mark-to-market accounting becomes a problem. Because the assets of a business are of a larger magnitude than its income or profits, when the income statement is attached to the balance sheet (through accounting rules), volatility increases.

For the economy as a whole, the ratio of total assets to profits and revenue has increased over time. When humans lived at subsistence, there were no assets, only income. We lived hand to mouth. But as people began to accumulate assets such as tools, weapons, and clothing, the ratio grew from near zero to a point where savings (asset accumulation) is much larger than gross domestic product (GDP).

Today, total accumulated U.S. assets (stocks, bonds, real estate, inventories, plant, and equipment), have reached roughly $150 trillion. This is the economy's balance sheet. However, it is GDP that represents the economy's income statement. This year that is roughly $15 trillion, or one-tenth the assets of the economy. A small ripple in the pool of assets (say 5 percent, or $7.5 trillion) can be a tsunami for the economy. In this scenario, the swing in asset values is equal to 50 percent of annual economic output.

This is why a pure version of mark-to-market accounting is such a damaging rule. Because it directly links assets to income, it increases volatility and creates a feedback loop that is highly pro-cyclical. It makes sharp booms and bubbles more likely, while also increasing the odds of panics and depressions. It is not a stretch to believe that it had a great deal to do with causing the Great Depression.

Milton Friedman and Anna Schwartz, in their seminal book *A Monetary History of the United States, 1867–1960*, wrote in 1963 (less than 30 years after the Great Depression) that:

> The *impairment in the market value* of assets held by banks, particularly in their bond portfolios, was *the most important source of impairment of capital leading to bank suspensions* [in the 1930s], rather than the default of specific loans or of specific bond issues.[8] [emphasis added]

While the response was late in coming, by 1938 regulators recognized the problem and suspended mark-to-market accounting. Since then, economic volatility has been damped significantly. Until 2008, the United States had avoided economic problems that even remotely resembled the panics and depressions of the prewar period. It is very difficult to "prove" that accounting rules alone helped damp the business cycle, but the coincidence is pretty darn spectacular, don't you think?

Of course, conventional wisdom does not give accounting rules any credit for a less volatile economy at all. It makes the assumption that government policy has calmed the business cycle. This view argues that the Fed's monetary policy and countercyclical government spending have made panics and depressions a thing of the past.

This view of the world presents a dilemma to its supporters. If government policy really does damp business cycles, how did the current crisis happen? Government is huge today, and the Fed cut rates right away. Their answer is that deregulation allowed it—that somehow the private sector got so out of control that it overwhelmed massive government spending and dramatic action by the Fed.

Many argue that the size and scope of the problem is directly related to the size and scope of the borrowing binge many Americans supposedly went on in the decades before the crisis. "No wonder the downturn is so painful," they argue. But the real problem is not deregulation, a lack of effort by the government, or the sins of consumers in the past; the real problem is mark-to-market accounting. It forced financial firms to take balance sheet losses into their income and capital statements.

What looked like a stable bank or investment bank yesterday looks like a sick bank today. When the value of a $150 trillion in assets begins to move around, it swamps GDP (income). Capital accounts don't stand a chance. They are overwhelmed by the sheer size of the balance sheet. And this is especially true when markets become illiquid.

Supporters of fair value accounting say it provides "transparency" and try to scare people by saying that without it, financial firms will make up any value they want when pricing assets. This is ludicrous. If anyone can say with a straight face that what happened in 2008 was transparent, they should be playing in the World Series of Poker. The financial system was about as clear as mud. If a small army of Fed and Treasury analysts, economists, and bureaucrats could not figure out what the appropriate value of Bear Stearns or Merrill Lynch was, what chance does an investor have (no matter what the accounting rules)?

Those supporters also cannot explain the 1980s, when the banking system was in much worse shape than in early 2008. As we saw in Chapter 5, the top eight banks (by asset size) in the United States had 263 percent of their capital lent to Latin American countries in the early 1980s. And every one of these countries defaulted. Latin American debt was trading at 10 cents on the dollar. In other words, every one of these banks was insolvent. Can you imagine what would have happened to the economy if these banks had been forced to close?

But because mark-to-market accounting did not exist, the government did not take them over. They were given time to work things out. As the late Bill Seidman, former head of the Federal Deposit Insurance Corporation (FDIC) wrote:

> . . . [I]n the case of Latin American loans, forbearance gave the lending banks time to make new arrangements with their debtors and meanwhile acquire enough capital so that losses on Latin American loans would not be fatal. Like medicine and the other healing arts, bank regulation is an art, not a science.[9]

This is why the economy grew and the stock market increased in the 1980s and 1990s despite the failure of thousands of banks and S&Ls. There are two important takeaways here. First, banks did not get to "make up" bond prices or hide from bad loans—thousands of them were forced to close their doors. Second, as they failed, the deleveraging and bank problems that so many fear right now did not destroy the economy.

Without mark-to-market accounting, the system had *time* to heal, which also allowed *growth* in the economy to lift the value of assets and reduce the size of problems. Mark-to-market accounting takes away both time and growth. It forces companies to take asset write-downs right now, with no time to work things out, and by destroying capital in the system it undermines the ability of risk takers to create opportunity.

Some say the market is the market, and if you want to own bonds, then you should be forced to mark them to market at all times. "This is the only way to truth," they say. And while this is understandable, it misses the point. There is always more than one price that makes sense.

Imagine a bank holds 1,000 individual mortgages; 300 of them have gone bad, but 700 are still paying on time. The bank has no intention or desire to sell any of these loans and marks those 300 bad loans to zero. At that point, the value of this book of business would be 70 cents on the dollar.

Then, imagine that those same 1,000 loans had been packaged together in a mortgage-backed security (bond). The same 300 loans had gone bad, but potential buyers are fearful that more loans will go bad. As a result, when auditors ask brokers for a bid in the open market, they get an offer of 40 cents on the dollar.

What we have then is a situation where there are two prices for a pool of assets (70 cents and 40 cents), and both of them are correct. One is priced by a holder who is willing to hold on and try to work things out. The other is priced by a market that is attempting to impute future value. While it may be true that the 40-cent bid turns out to be correct, it is also true that marking the assets down to this price *before* 300 additional mortgages really do go bad wipes out 30 cents of bank capital that does not need to be wiped out. This in turn could undermine economic activity, making it more likely that unemployment will rise and more people will default on their mortgages.

In fact, if the write-downs are severe enough in a distressed marketplace, the practice of mark-to-market accounting could wipe out the entire banking system and cause a calamity. The marketplace for bonds and stocks is a discounting mechanism. Forcing the current economy to take hits (or gifts) that may or may not ever come about is a recipe for volatility, confusion, bubbles, and busts.

A simple example can elucidate the problem. Imagine that you live in a million-dollar home in the hills above Santa Barbara, California, and you have a $600,000 mortgage. And then imagine that there is a forest fire two miles from your house and the Santa Ana winds are blowing it your way.

Now let's imagine that your banker knocks on your door and says, "We need to mark this house to market right now. What do you think your house is worth with a fire just two miles away—how about $200,000?" The banker then says you need to come up with $440,000 right now. That way you can end up with a $160,000 mortgage on a $200,000 house. If you can't come up with the money, you lose your house and you are declared bankrupt. Even if the wind shifts direction that afternoon, it's too late. You've already been marked to market.

This is what was happening to banks in 2008. Accountants, with the authority of government behind them, were forcing banks to price assets to the bid price even if there was no market. Banks were not given time to see if the fire missed them; they were not allowed to price assets to actual cash flow; and there was no attempt to figure out whether market prices were based on cash flow, a pessimistic assumption of future performance, or just lowball bids from short-sellers who were trying to drive companies out of business.

By the way, this was one reason no bank in their right mind would become transparent about what they actually owned. If they did, short-sellers would know exactly what securities to put lowball bids on in an attempt to drive the stock price down. In this process, the short-sellers found allies in the press to complain that there was no transparency. Short-sellers wanted more transparency so that they could break the banks over the knee of mark-to-market accounting.

Suspend Mark-to-Market

This is why the only real answer to this problem is the full suspension of mark-to-market accounting. If we do not suspend it, if we continue to let it hang in the air, then markets for potentially volatile and illiquid securities could cease to exist, or at least shrink dramatically in size. Why would anyone buy a pool of securitized assets as a long-term investment in a mark-to-market world? The very nature of securitized assets is that they could end up being valued at well below the true cash flow of the underlying loans in the pool.

Nonetheless, short-sellers and apologists for fair value accounting yell loudly whenever anyone suggests suspending the rule. They argue that the United States would turn into Japan if we suspended fair value accounting and that banks could put any price on their assets that they wanted. They have argued that we would give up transparency. They complain that the stock market would fall if we suspended mark-to-market accounting because no one would trust the banks. And they argue that banks knew the rules and they should therefore pay the consequences.

The one about Japan is a huge stretch meant to imply a "lost decade" of economic growth if the United States rescinded fair value accounting. But Japanese banks had problems because they refused to write-down loans that were already in default and would never repay. No one who supports suspension of mark-to-market accounting believes that banks in the United States should be allowed to do that. Mark-to-market accounting is extreme; it forces banks to write down assets even if the underlying loans are still being paid in full and on time.

The last objection about strictly following rules is perhaps the most idiotic. Imagine that your seven-year-old son talks back to his mom. Dad puts him in a one-hour time-out, but 15 minutes later realizes that the house is on fire. So Dad gets the family organized to leave the house, stops by to see his 7-year-old on the way out and says, "Son, you knew the rules before you talked back to your mom. We are all leaving because the house is on fire, but you need to finish your time-out. Good luck!"

Any father who behaved this way would be considered insane. And if the boy got hurt, the father would find himself in court. Two wrongs do not make a right. In normal times, when markets are functioning, there is no problem with mark-to-market accounting. But when markets shut down, when the world catches on fire, the rule needs to be suspended—that's just common sense.

Unfortunately, because this decision is left up to government bureaucrats and accountants, they cannot be trusted to make the right decision. Accountants do not have responsibility for the businesses that they audit. They are not owners. However, because the government destroyed Arthur Andersen over Enron, auditors have been forced—or at least believe they can be forced—to take liability. Liability for the outcome without responsibility for the results is a recipe for disaster.

Running a business takes both objective and subjective decision making. Accountants, or anyone with the liability of a business's action but no responsibility for the outcome, do not want to make subjective decisions. Only objective and measurable decisions can be backed up in a court of law or the court of public opinion. Subjective decisions can be argued and explained, but with hindsight can always be picked apart.

Just look at what has happened in recent years. There is no way that I will ever believe that the owners and managers of Bear Stearns, Lehman Brothers, AIG, or many other financial institutions that got into trouble chose to bet their companies on a roll of the dice. Many of the executives had their life's savings (and their life's work) wrapped up in these firms.

It has been reported that Jimmy Cayne, who worked at Bear Stearns from 1969 until 2008, and became the firm's president in 1985, saw his net worth fall from nearly $1 billion to just $60 million when the firm failed. Virtually his entire personal fortune was in the stock of the company. To believe that he "bet the farm" on subprime mortgages is to ignore his entire life's work. The conventional wisdom—that it was all about greed and avarice—just doesn't make sense.

Cayne and executives at other firms made many subjective decisions, but they also made many objective decisions (some based on the Fed's artificially low rates). Yet they have been tried and convicted in the court of public opinion. Conventional wisdom says they were greedy jerks and they put the entire economy at risk to enrich themselves. But this is a guilty verdict based on 20/20 hindsight. No accountant wants to be put in this spot.

As a result, mark-to-market accounting is the perfect tool for accountants. All they need to do is get three bids, document the process, and then pick the middle one. But this process is crazy in an illiquid market. The prices we obtain in the bidding process have no relationship to the current value of the securities, based on cash flow, we are attempting to price. In many cases, there were many lowball bids for securities, but no actual trades for months at a time. How should those lowball bids ever be trusted to reflect the true marketplace?

In fact, the lowball bids were partly due to the impact of mark-to-market accounting. If I know that banks will be forced to write down the value of their assets to levels well below the value based on cash flows, why not put a low-ball bid in place? The bank will be forced to take the loss either way, so maybe I can pick up some distressed assets at really cheap prices. This process, and fair value accounting, drove many very good firms right out of existence.

A False Feeling of Control

Before we get to the good news, it is important to think about what mark-to-market accounting is really all about. It is an attempt to have everything in the world objective and measurable and transparent. It is an attempt to take the risk out of life. But life is full of risk, and trying to take the risk out is a recipe for mediocrity. Without risk taking, there is no growth.

If you lived your life thinking about risk, you might never leave your house. After all, you might get hit by a bus, even if you lived on a cul-de-sac or your town didn't have buses (because a bus might get lost). This, of course, would be ludicrous, but that is what these accounting rules and regulations are really all about: pricing everything to a market price, as if doing so would alleviate all risk.

But this doesn't alleviate risk. When subprime mortgages were first being manufactured and then securitized, the rating agencies rated the loans triple-A and house prices were rising 8 percent or more per year. These loans were marked up during that period because the market did not reflect the true risk. And then, when the market dried up and only lowball bids were found in highly illiquid markets, the marked-down price was well below true value.

Accounting values are only estimates. For example, if the computer on your desk is over three years old, it is valued on the books of the company at zero because it is depreciated over a three-year period. But if it still works, it is worth more than zero. And if an airline hedges its fuel costs, it must write the hedge to market value at the end of every quarter even if the hedge has years to run. But if fuel costs fall and the carrier knows it will save money over the next six months, it is not allowed to book those lower costs until they happen.

Mark-to-market accounting may appear to provide some kind of super-truth, but in reality it is a false feeling of control. More importantly, it is a very dangerous concept when markets become illiquid and volatile and when accounting values can affect regulatory capital ratios. Then the rule creates more problems than it could possibly ever solve, even in a perfect world.

A Miracle Happened

No matter how persuasive the arguments made here, there will be many who disagree about the role of mark-to-market accounting in causing the Panic of 2008. But those denials now have a huge hurdle to overcome. After many false starts, the FASB was finally forced to alter fair value accounting rules in 2009.

The congressional hearing that changed everything took place on March 12, 2009, but was announced about a week before. This, as it turns out, coincides perfectly with the bottom of the stock market decline. On March 9, 2009 with the Dow at 6,547 and the S&P 500 trading at 667, the rally started.

The final changes from FASB were announced on April 2, 2009. The accountants said that in the case of illiquid markets, an institution could use "cash flow" to value assets. This was enough to end the bank capital crisis. No longer were banks, or investors in banks, at risk of having an accounting rule wipe out the institution. Bank managers now had an ability to fight it out with auditors who would take only bids in the marketplace as any sign of true value.

The fact that the market bottomed in mid-March and moved up is in direct contradiction to short-sellers who argued that weakening mark-to-market accounting would cause stock prices to fall because investors, especially foreign ones, would no longer trust the U.S. markets. They were very, very wrong. Not only did the stock market soar 40 percent in just two months, but financial companies in the United States raised nearly $100 billion in capital in just a few weeks once mark-to-market rules were altered. Moreover, all those Treasury and Fed programs that were designed to take illiquid assets off of bank balance sheets found themselves with little to do.

It would still be better if mark-to-market were suspended. It is hard to imagine that a fully functioning securitization marketplace will come back in the years ahead if potential investors believe that this accounting rule will return. The FASB has not given up and is now trying to apply mark-to-market accounting to all assets of a financial institution, even loans. There is no real market for bank loans, and the value of any loan is always in the eye of the beholder. As a result, "who" is doing the beholding determines the prices of loans and possibly the viability of an institution, and maybe even the health of the economy.

If that power is given to accountants, who have no actual responsibility for running financial institutions but can be tarred with some of the liability, the result will be a more tentative banking system that takes less risk. That may sound good these days, but imagine watching a football game played by accountants who stop running because they might get a broken leg when tackled. Fair value accounting needs to be fully suspended—now.

But even without full suspension, the reform of mark-to-market that happened in April, when combined with a super-easy monetary policy and the end of an economic panic that started in September, is working to lift the economy and the markets out of the ashes of the Panic of 2008. The winners are banks, surviving financial institutions of all types, and cyclical companies. The losers are the short-sellers who actually believe what they argued. The stock market rally that began in March 2009 will not be over until a few short-only hedge funds go belly-up.

Chapter 7

Panic and the Speed of Money

Economists are not psychologists. But it doesn't take a shrink to understand why people are so ready to believe that the world, or at least the economy as we know it, is coming to an end.

Even before any problems with subprime loans, just about every company and every job in America was at risk of being taken out by some new invention, or by the productivity improvements that come from those inventions. As discussed in Chapter 3, the world is in the middle of a technological transformation more powerful than the industrial revolution. Despite the fact that these technological changes will boost living standards over the long run, it is no fun for those caught up in the destructive side of creative destruction.

While some people roll with the punches, many see only pain and misfortune. And with politicians ready to blame any pain that people feel on capitalism or the greedy rich, no wonder people started to think that something fundamental was wrong with the economy. As was also true at the turn of the last century—when farming gave way to urban life—transformational change was considered unfair and unjust. And these feelings led to an increase in populist political sentiment.

Today, this natural political pressure is compounded by the fact that journalism is at the center of the storm. The *New York Times*, *Chicago Tribune*, *Washington Post*, and *Los Angeles Times*, along with just about every other major newspaper, have seen circulation and ad revenue plummet. Craigslist has taken over a huge part of classified advertising, while the Internet has promoted an endless set of alternative news sources. At the same time, the big three television networks have seen their audience eroded by cable alternatives.

Despite denials, these financial problems absolutely must affect journalists' perceptions of the economy and therefore the news coverage. This is different than political bias. It's just reality. In an environment where coworkers are losing their jobs, pay and hours are being cut, and the fear of bankruptcy is in the air, journalists would not be human if they were not affected. A dour slant on the news is understandable.

Add to this the fact that politicians of all stripes are fanning economic pessimism in an attempt to gain political advantage. Liberals want national health care and a tax on carbon (to save the world). They paint a very dour picture of our environment and health care system, and they say that fixing them is essential for creating long-term economic growth. Conservatives paint the economy as terrible so that they can tar the Obama administration with any fallout.

It's a party for negative thinkers, and the economy has played its role. The housing market is in its worst shape since the Great Depression, very well known companies have failed, the unemployment rate is up sharply, and the stock market got crushed just when baby boomers were getting ready to retire. It's no wonder people are scared, mad, and confused about what happened and what will happen. It's easy to convince people that capitalism has failed.

Call it "The Great Confluence." Every single significant interest group—the citizen, the press, liberals, conservatives, short-sellers, and even typically optimistic people—have a reason to be pessimistic.

Anyone who is truly optimistic, like the author of this book, is looked at like they have three eyes. But the fact that you have made it this far suggests that you might be willing to listen to ideas that are different from the conventional wisdom. So here's a big one: It is highly probable that the U.S. economy could have avoided a recession altogether, or at least the downturn would have been shallow and short like the 2000–2001 recession, if the government had not made mistakes. This recession was not caused by a failure of capitalism. Capitalism was working just fine, and it could have handled the financial problems of recent years on its own, with much less damage, panic, and fear than actually occurred.

What Recession?

Look, I know that it's hard to imagine the United States could have avoided a recession. Nouriel Roubini, along with other bears and many short-sellers, have already been inducted into the forecasting Hall of Fame. The pouting pundits of pessimism treat many of these bears like royalty. Many believe that they were right about the collapse of housing, the shadow banking system, debt levels, leverage—everything.

But were they? A look at the actual data suggests they were technically right (the economy did fall into recession and the market did go down), but they were right for the wrong reasons. The recession did not happen because housing collapsed; it happened because the government bought into the pessimism and made huge mistakes and scared everyone half to death.

Housing sales peaked way back in 2005, while residential construction and home prices peaked in 2006. In other words, the housing market was in free fall for at least two or three years before the economy fell into recession. The economy was losing jobs in early 2008, but when Lehman Brothers failed and the Troubled Asset Repurchase Plan (TARP) was first announced by Bush Treasury Secretary Hank Paulson, the economy collapsed. The most serious drop in activity did not happen until September 2008. In other words, what the short-sellers and Dr. Doom said would cause a recession—the collapse of housing—did not drag down overall economic growth in real time. There was a very long lag, and it took government mismanagement to help turn what was an economic problem into an utter catastrophe.

In the fourth quarter of 2005, housing peaked at 6.3 percent of gross domestic product (GDP). This was more than 37 percent above the 10-year (1985–1995) average of 4.6 percent. Two years later, in the fourth quarter of 2007, housing had fallen to just 3.9 percent of GDP. Since then, it has declined even more, and as of the second quarter of 2009 was just 2.4 percent of GDP, about one-half its normal level, where it seemingly has bottomed (see Figure 7.1).

In 2006 and 2007, the economy suffered greatly from this slump in housing. The economy lost 125,000 construction jobs between the peak in early 2006 and late 2007. By December 2007, residential construction activity had fallen by more than a third from its all-time high in March 2006 (from an annual rate of $676 billion to $414 billion). At the same time, retail sales of building materials fell by 13 percent between early 2006 and the end of 2007. All of this represented the worst declines on record—maybe even as bad as the Great Depression.

But the economy avoided recession. All those forecasters that said the economy would collapse as housing collapsed were proven wrong.

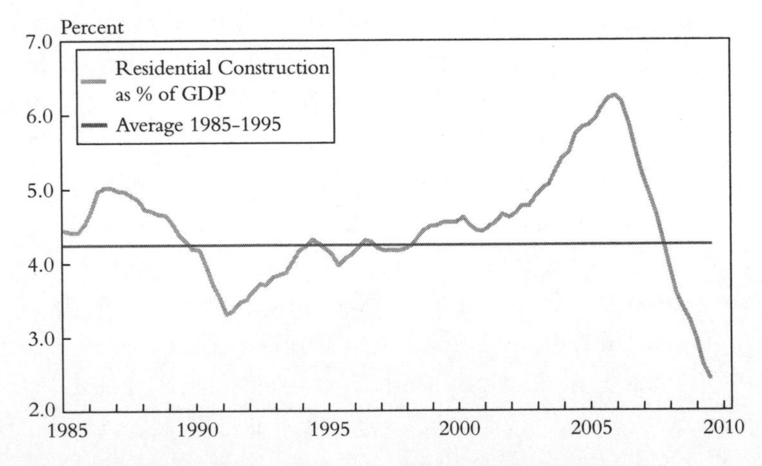

Figure 7.1 Residential Construction as a Percentage of GDP
SOURCE: Bureau of Economic Analysis

Even with housing in a free fall during 2006–2007, real GDP still grew 2.5 percent at an annual rate. Excluding housing, real GDP growth was 3.7 percent—a boom. This meant 96 percent of economic activity (what is left after excluding housing) was still growing faster than the past 50-year average growth rate of 3.4 percent.

This does not mean there were no problems. Housing was a clear drag on the economy and gasoline prices were surging. Unemployment was rising, even though it was still well below 6 percent right up through the summer of 2008. On January 7, 2008, the National Bureau of Economic Research (NBER) released a statement that said there wasn't enough evidence of an economic downturn to declare an official recession.

At that time, this was the correct call. Housing continued to fall, but the rest of the economy remained strong. Even though overall real GDP fell slightly in the first quarter of 2008 (by 0.7 percent at an annual rate), it rebounded in the second quarter to a growth rate of 1.5 percent.

Excluding housing, the picture was even brighter. As can be seen in Figure 7.2, nonhousing real GDP grew at a 3.8 percent annual rate in the fourth quarter of 2007, and then proceeded to expand at a 0.6 percent growth rate in the first quarter of 2008 and 2.2 percent in the second

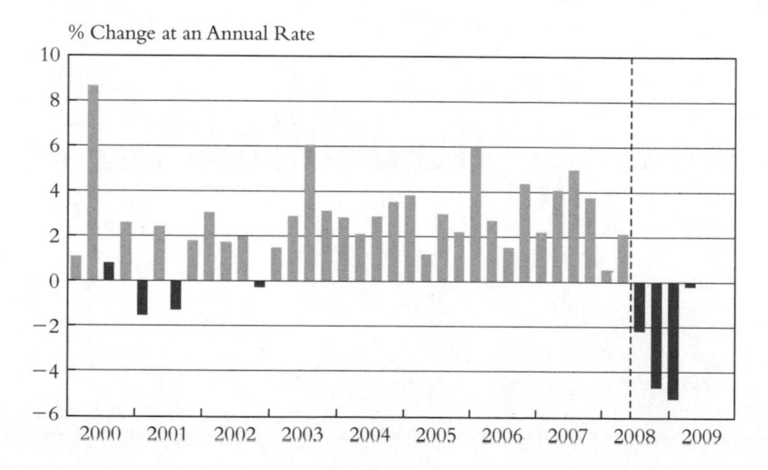

Figure 7.2 Real GDP Excluding Housing
SOURCE: Bureau of Economic Analysis

quarter. It was not until the third quarter of 2008 that both overall and nonhousing real GDP fell.

The Panic of 2008

The NBER eventually picked December 2007 as the end of the recovery that began in November 2001. The NBER uses a combination of data on consumer spending, employment, incomes, and production to make these calls. So, despite the fact that the nonhousing economy was still growing strongly in December and for at least six months into 2008, there are significant signs that the economy had turned down.

Considering the wreckage of mark-to-market on the lending markets, the weakness in housing and the surge in oil prices to $145 per barrel in 2008, the recession was relatively muted at first. Overall real GDP fell just 0.7 percent at an annual rate in the first three quarters of 2008. And, as can be seen in Figure 7.3, nominal consumer spending did not decline until the fourth quarter. In other words, the calamity many were expecting from the decline in housing did not show up until the early fall of 2008.

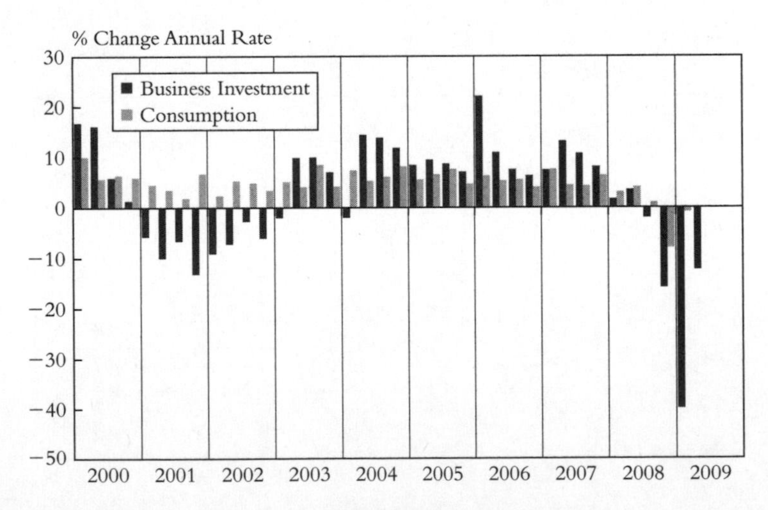

Figure 7.3 Consumer Spending and Business Investment
SOURCE: Bureau of Economic Analysis, Quarterly Annualized Changes

It was September 2008 when the proverbial stuff hit the fan. An item-by-item timeline is basically useless because there will be differences of opinion about what actually happened as long as there are people around and they have time to debate. But one thing that almost everyone can agree with is that when the Treasury and Fed decided to let Lehman Bothers fail on September 15, 2008, the game changed.

Panic began to spread. A $65 billion money market fund, the Reserve Primary Fund, became the first money market fund open to the general public in history to "break the buck."[1] The fund held $785 million of commercial paper issued by Lehman Brothers. As fears about safety and soundness spread, more than $170 billion was withdrawn from money market mutual funds in one week. People even began to mistrust banks, and some withdrew cash from well-capitalized community banks out of pure fear.

Four days later, on Friday, September 19, Hank Paulson proposed the $700 billion TARP, telling Congress in a series of private meetings that the United States was on the cusp of collapse and that a "major" financial institution was about to fail. It's hard to put this in context when today's deficits are counted in the trillions, but back then $700 billion was a lot of money. Congress was shocked by its size, and scared (but not quite convinced) by Paulson's fear-mongering.

Despite all of this, the initial TARP, just a simple three-page document, was consumed by debate. The Bush administration wanted a vote on the following Monday, September 22, 2008. But that vote did not happen until a week later. The bill swelled to over 100 pages, but lost, 228–205 in the U.S. House of Representatives on September 29, 2009. The Dow fell 7 percent, nearly 778 points on that day, the biggest one-day point drop in history. The S&P 500 fell 9 percent, the third biggest decline since World War II.

It sounded and felt like Armageddon. "This is panic and . . . fear run amok," Zachary Karabell, president of River Twice Research, told CNBC. "Right now we are in a classic moment of a financial meltdown," he said.[2] "You just felt like the world was unraveling," Ryan Larson, senior equity trader at Voyageur Asset Management, told the *New York Times*.[3]

At the same time all of this was happening, the Federal Reserve was making announcements left and right. One day after Lehman was allowed to fail, the Federal Open Market Committee met and held its federal funds rate at 2 percent. Two days later, on Thursday, the Fed and five other central banks announced $427 billion in reciprocal currency arrangements (swap lines). On Friday, the day TARP was first proposed, the Fed said it would buy commercial paper from money market funds. On Sunday, it approved the applications of Goldman Sachs and Morgan Stanley to become bank holding companies.

As if all this weren't enough to stir up real fear about the economy, on September 24, 2008, President Bush gave a prime-time speech, just a few days before TARP failed in the house. In that TV spectacle, he said:

> We're in the midst of a serious financial crisis . . . major sectors of America's financial system are at risk of shutting down. . . . The government's top economic experts warn that, without immediate action by Congress, America could slip into a financial panic and a distressing scenario would unfold.
>
> More banks could fail, including some in your community. The stock market would drop even more, which would reduce the value of your retirement account. The value of your home could plummet. Foreclosures would rise dramatically.
>
> And if you own a business or a farm, you would find it harder and more expensive to get credit. More businesses would close their doors, and millions of Americans could lose their jobs.[4]

This might have been one of the worst speeches by a president ever in history. The only one remotely as bad was Jimmy Carter's fireside chat in 1977; while wearing a light brown cardigan sweater, he told Americans that we were about to run out of oil and that our future would be one of high unemployment and inflation.

President Bush said we had faced challenges before and that "we will overcome this one."[5] This was kind of surreal. When the president of the United States says you could lose your house, your pension, and your job, but then says, don't panic . . . PEOPLE PANIC.

There was a run on Washington Mutual, a major Seattle-based bank, with $16 billion withdrawn over a 10-day period. And on September 25, 2008, the day after President Bush's speech, it was taken over by the Federal Deposit Insurance Corporation (FDIC). This led to even more support for the TARP plan.

All of a sudden, economic activity plummeted. In economic terms, the velocity of money—the turnover of money—declined. In the United States, this type of panic had not happened for over 100 years. The Panic of 1907, after the San Francisco earthquake, was the last time a panic took the U.S. economy down.

Velocity is a concept in monetary theory that describes how one dollar of money can lead to many more dollars of economic activity over time. If you spend money at Walgreens, it finds its way back to the bank, and then the bank puts the money into an ATM machine and then someone else takes it out and spends it at Starbucks. Each year, every dollar creates a multiple of its worth in economic activity.

One simple way of measuring this is to take GDP and divide it by the money supply. In Figure 7.4, this has been done with GDP

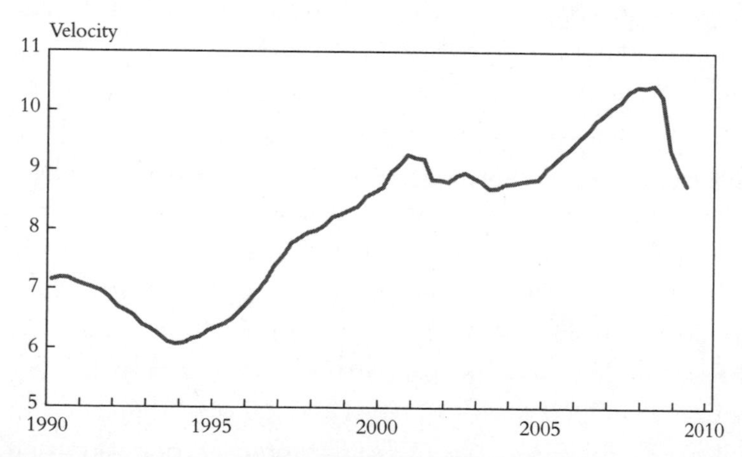

Figure 7.4 Velocity of Money: GDP Divided by M1
SOURCE: Bureau of Economic Analysis, Federal Reserve Board

and M-1 (Money One—which includes cash, checking accounts, and traveler's checks). The velocity of M-1, the amount of times each dollar is spent per year, fell slightly from 10.5 in the second quarter of 2008, to 10.3 in the third quarter. Since the panic did not start until mid-September, the third quarter showed little impact. But then things got ugly. Velocity fell to 9.4 in the fourth quarter of 2008, 9.1 in the first quarter of 2009, and then finally to 8.8 during the second quarter of 2009.

A drop in velocity is a direct hit to spending, and in this case velocity fell roughly 16 percent from its peak to its trough. The drop in economic activity was astounding. In the fourth quarter of 2008, overall food sales—yes, food sales—fell at a 10 percent annualized rate. Grocery store sales fell 9.8 percent at an annual rate between September and December. This means that people decided to eat out of their pantries rather than go out for dinner or even go to the grocery store. This is an extremely rare occurrence.

Car and truck sales plummeted to a 9.0 million annual rate. With 240 million cars and trucks on the road, this sales pace meant that vehicles would be replaced only once every 26 years. Even in the nasty recessions of the early 1980s, the sales pace bottomed at a 16-year replacement rate. At the early 2009 sales pace, the United States was not even replacing the 13 million or so vehicles that were totaled or just died of old age each year. This could not last.

And housing, which had been showing some signs of life in mid-2008, experienced another leg down. Existing home sales had seemingly bottomed in April 2008 at an annual rate of 4.85 million units. They then climbed three out of five months between April and September, to 5.1 million, 5.2 percent above the April lows. But then the panic struck.

Housing starts fell 40 percent between September 2008 and January 2009—to just 488,000 units at an annual rate. With 130 million houses in America, this pace of new starts meant that it would take more than 260 years to replace them all. Typically, housing stock is replaced every 65 to 70 years. Moreover, population growth, fires, and just worn-out buildings mean that the United States needs to build 1.6 million new homes a year just to keep up. With starts below

500,000, the building industry was not even close to levels necessary for normal life in America.

These levels of activity suggest that something different happened. This was not a normal, run-of-the-mill, tight-monetary-policy-induced recession. It was panic. The best economic explanation is that it was a drop in the velocity of money. In our modern era, these types of recessions are nonexistent. We haven't seen anything like it in 100 years. Nonetheless, it was a very nasty recession. No longer was the nonhousing economy absorbing the losses in the housing sector.

Mark-to-Market Mayhem

At the time the government decided to let Lehman Brothers fail, there were many people—including Steve Forbes, Newt Gingrich, and William Isaac (a former head of the FDIC in the 1980s), and myself—who were pointing out the damaging nature of mark-to-market accounting.

While Chapter 6 was devoted to this issue, it is important to bring it back up here, because this was the point at which it did the maximum damage. The Bush administration ignored anyone who talked about mark-to-market and stuck to its guns. It wanted to bail out banks rather than let them work their own way out. The original TARP proposal was designed to buy up the toxic assets on bank balance sheets so that the erosion in their prices would stop the hemorrhaging of bank capital. In the president's September 24 speech, he made this point clear:

> . . . [A]s markets have lost confidence in mortgage-backed securities, their prices have dropped sharply, yet *the value of many of these assets will likely be higher than their current price, because the vast majority of Americans will ultimately pay off their mortgages.*
>
> The government is the one institution with the patience and resources to buy these assets at their current low prices and hold them until markets return to normal.

> And when that happens, money will flow back to the Treasury as these assets are sold, and we expect that much, if not all, of the tax dollars we invest will be paid back.[6] [emphasis added]

The government knew the market was undervaluing these securities. The president said this straight out. But the real problem wasn't that the prices were too low; the real problem was that banks were being forced to take those illiquid market quotes and the losses that they created and push them through the balance sheet as a hit to regulatory capital. It had nothing to do with "patience" or "resources." Banks were threatened with insolvency because of accounting rules. This created uncertainty in the market, chased away private capital, and put banks that might not have faced difficultly otherwise in the direct line of fire.

It didn't take a rocket scientist to know, even before the TARP bill was voted on, that no bank would sell these toxic assets at prices they thought were too low. Almost immediately, the government had to change its plan. Exactly when does not really matter, but very soon after passage on October 3, or maybe even before, Hank Paulson knew that he would use the TARP funds to put capital directly into banks rather than buy up toxic assets.

The problem was never the toxic assets themselves, but the accounting rules. Private capital did not trust banks that owned significant amounts of toxic assets, not because actual losses from those securities would lead to bankruptcy, but because accounting rules threatened to destroy capital, and possibly the banks themselves, as long as the markets were illiquid. Private capital went on strike. And when that happened, the money dried up. No one will ever know what would have happened if the government had changed mark-to-market accounting earlier, but it is not out of the realm of possibility that Lehman Brothers, Bear Stearns, Washington Mutual, and Wachovia may not have failed.

Despite arguments to the contrary, the White House, the Treasury Department, and the Federal Reserve continued to support mark-to-market accounting. While it is always possible that they were blind to the glaringly obvious problems caused by this accounting rule, it is more likely that they used the rule to maintain control over the banking system. This was disastrous.

Because the government would not change the accounting rules and because banks would not participate in the TARP, Treasury Secretary Paulson called the major banks of the United States to the Treasury on October 13, 2008. At that meeting, he forced those banks to take $150 billion of government money as direct investments in their financial institutions. This abuse of government power caused even more concern in financial markets.

What might be most interesting about all of this is that many normally stalwart supporters of free markets argued against changing mark-to-market rules and basically applauded the heavy hand of government. For the rest of my life, I will never understand why this was the case. But the best explanation is that they panicked, they lost their cool, and they bought into the government's view of the situation, that only government could solve the problem. They completely forgot about the 1980s and 1990s, when the economy absorbed much larger problems with ease.

With the economy in free fall, the government using a very heavy hand, and panic in the air, the economy and stock market continued to fall. Real GDP collapsed by 5.4 percent at an annual rate in the fourth quarter of 2008 and 6.4 percent in the first quarter of 2009. The S&P 500 fell 48 percent from August 28, 2008, to March 9, 2009, while the Dow fell 44 percent.

Short-sellers made billions, Nouriel Roubini and other bearish forecasters became heroes, and the government solidified its hold on the financial system. Senator Barack Obama won the presidential election in a populist landslide, and the capitalist system took the fall for what was clearly an astounding set of government mistakes.

AIG, Credit Default Swaps, and Derivatives

Despite all of this activity, what became the poster child, the quintessential company, for all of this mayhem was American International Group (AIG)—founded in 1919 and one of the largest public companies in the world. Just one day after the Treasury and Fed decided not to save Lehman Brothers, they decided to support AIG, with an $85 billion credit facility arguing that it was truly "too big—or perhaps too interconnected—to fail."[7]

AIG was the biggest player in the market for credit default swaps (CDSs)—insurance for the bond market. Let's say a pension fund owned $10 million of Exxon debt and wanted to insure itself against the loss of principal. It could pay AIG a premium (say 0.5 percent, or $50,000 per year) to do so. If Exxon went bankrupt, and the pension fund collected only $3 million on its bonds, AIG would pay $7 million to make up the difference—the loss.

Most bonds AIG insured were normal, investment-grade corporate debt. But in the early 2000s, it started to insure consumer debt, including subprime mortgages. In 2005, however, once AIG became worried that this market had become too risky, it stopped insuring those types of bonds. Still, they held billions on the books.

As long as AIG maintained its triple-A rating, it did not need to post extra collateral to back these transactions. It could collect premiums and maintain capital ratios like any insurance company. But if AIG's credit rating was reduced, or in some cases if the value of the bonds it insured fell, it would be forced to put more collateral aside. The terms of the collateral—a percentage of the value of its CDS contracts—were negotiated for each transaction.

At the peak, it is estimated that AIG held roughly $520 billion in default swaps—$450 billion of these swaps on typical, investment-grade corporate bonds, and $75 billion on consumer debt, including subprime and Alt-A mortgage bonds. It was the mortgage-backed securities that initially caused problems at AIG. As the housing market declined and delinquencies increased, the value of mortgage-backed securities began to fall.

And as President Bush said, these mortgage bonds were priced well below their true value based on the actual performance of the underlying mortgages. The market had become illiquid, and prices plummeted. To top it off, auditors were forcing AIG and every other financial firm to price their financial contracts to these outrageously low prices. This ballooned losses at AIG, which led to the lowering of its credit rating. This created a vicious downward spiral.

The Fed and Treasury tried to negotiate an injection of private capital, but they could find no one to help. As long as mark-to-market accounting was in place, why in the world would any private entity put money into a black hole? No matter how low prices for mortgage-backed securities had fallen, they could still fall more. Finally, the government stepped in with its $85 billion.

But this was just the beginning. As panic spread, the prices for CDSs on regular investment-grade corporate debt—even U.S. Treasury debt—began to skyrocket. In early December 2008, it cost $60 per year to insure $10,000 in U.S. Treasury debt for five years, which was up from $8 a year earlier and $36 in November. This was crazy. The odds of America's defaulting on its debt are nil, the government can always print money to pay off its bonds. In other words, the market was pricing in absolute Armageddon (as in: maybe the printing presses wouldn't work anymore). Make that quadruple or quintuple Armageddon.

The worst default rates in history for investment-grade debt are less than 10 percent. But, the market started pricing in 40–50 percent default rates. This opened up a chasm in AIG's balance sheet as big as the Grand Canyon. As fear of defaults rose, AIG's mark-to-market losses rose, which in turn increased the threat to the economy, which raised the fear of defaults even more.

The result was that the Treasury and the Fed were forced to raise their stake in AIG to $182 billion in order to fill the hole. This money was almost immediately paid out to other private banks around the world, which owned the other side of the bond insurance contracts. This was the deal that AIG had agreed to when writing many of these contracts.

Without mark-to-market accounting, the value of mortgage bonds and default swaps would probably never have fallen this much and AIG would never have taken such huge losses. But because of it, a vicious cycle had begun. The bigger the write-downs and the more government money was shoveled into AIG, the more fear grew and the more illiquid the market became. When this was combined with the economic panic and the drop in the velocity of money, it became very easy to believe that the end had come.

In the midst of all this, Bernie Madoff's $60 billion Ponzi scheme (the largest in history) was discovered, and Allen Stanford, chairman of Stanford Financial Group, was charged with fraud totaling $8 billion. While some people want to put all of this into one big pot and stir it up, Stanford and Madoff do not represent the capitalist system, unless you want to blame capitalism for human nature. But even in socialist systems, crooks exist.

Nonetheless, at the height of the panic, capitalism and investment banking became four-letter words. There was a real fear that the economy might never come back again.

The V-Shaped Light at the End of the Tunnel

But the capitalist system is more resilient than almost anyone believes. Just when everyone had lost hope, and even before mark-to-market accounting rules were changed, retail sales leapt 1.7 percent in January, after falling at an annualized rate of 29 percent in the final three months of 2008. And once they turned, retail sales traced out a V-shaped recovery (see Figure 7.5). The Baltic Freight Index, a cost index for shipping dry bulk cargo such as grains, plummeted in late 2008, but rose 300 percent in the first six months of 2009.

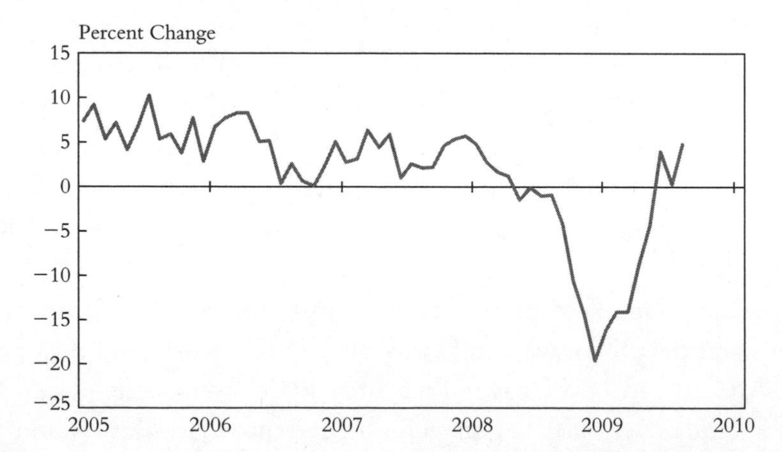

Figure 7.5 Growth in Retail Sales: Six-Month Annualized Percent Change
SOURCE: Census Bureau

Perhaps the best picture of what happened is the price of copper. It has been an important commodity to the world for centuries and is sometimes called the "metal with a PhD in economics," because its price movement often mirrors overall economic activity. As Figure 7.6 shows, it was trading in a range between $3 and $4 a pound for years, but then plummeted to roughly $1/lb. in mid-September 2008, after Lehman Brothers failed and TARP was proposed. But, starting in early 2009 it began a V-shaped rally, with its price more than doubling in the first half of the year as the economy began to recover.

On March 9, 2009, the stock market bottomed as well, with the S&P 500 rising 40 percent in three months and three days. In that same time period, the Nasdaq Composite rose 47 percent, to 1,862. This was a far cry from the 5,000 peak back in March 2000, but it was clear that the panic was over. Spreads between corporate bonds and Treasury bonds, and swap spreads—both measures of the appetite for risk in the bond market—began to narrow as well.

The pouting pundits of pessimism and the short-sellers were still not convinced that the economy was getting better, but the data were reflecting an improved atmosphere. And this wasn't that hard to

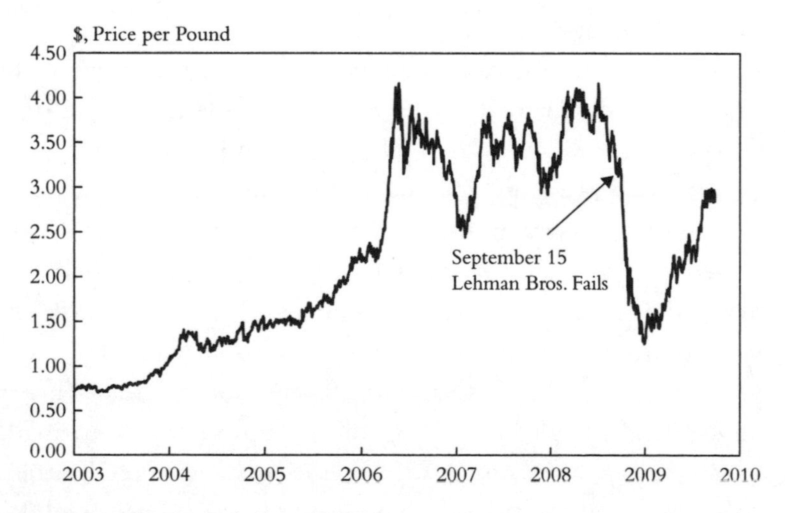

Figure 7.6 Copper Price per Pound
SOURCE: Commodity Research Bureau

understand. There were three things lifting the economy and markets in early 2009.

First, and probably most important for economic growth, was that the Fed was running an extremely accommodative monetary policy. Not only was the Fed holding the federal funds rate well below nominal GDP, but it was also directly buying bonds in the open market to expand its balance sheet. Money numbers were exploding.

The textbook response to a drop in the velocity of money is for the Federal Reserve to print more money. If people are spending money more slowly, then putting more money in the economy will offset the drop. Back in 1907, there was no Federal Reserve Board—it didn't come into existence until 1913. So the only way for the economy to heal was for the panic to subside. These days, because the Fed exists, and because it did become more accommodative, it can offset the panic.

The Fed cut the federal funds rate twice, by 50 basis points each time, in October 2008. This pushed the rate to 1.0 percent. But as the panic worsened, the Fed cut the funds rate one more time, to a range of between 0 percent and 0.25 percent in December. At this point the Fed was running the most accommodative peacetime policy in its 96-year history. And this alone was enough to offset the damage done by the drop in velocity.

Second, the panic had run its course; human nature suggests that people won't stay down for long. A more up-to-date estimate of the velocity of M-1 can be calculated by using monthly data on personal consumption. And as Figure 7.7 shows, M-1 velocity (at least relative to consumption) stabilized in the early part of 2009. As long as velocity is stabilizing, then any increases in the money supply will boost economic activity. And if velocity accelerates again, what the United States will experience is a turbocharged economic growth rate.

And third, the U.S. Congress finally forced the Financial Accounting Standards Board (FASB) to let up on mark-to-market accounting. As we have noted before, the stock market bottomed at the same time mark-to-market accounting was being reformed. Risk spreads in the bond market retreated sharply, the credit markets opened up,

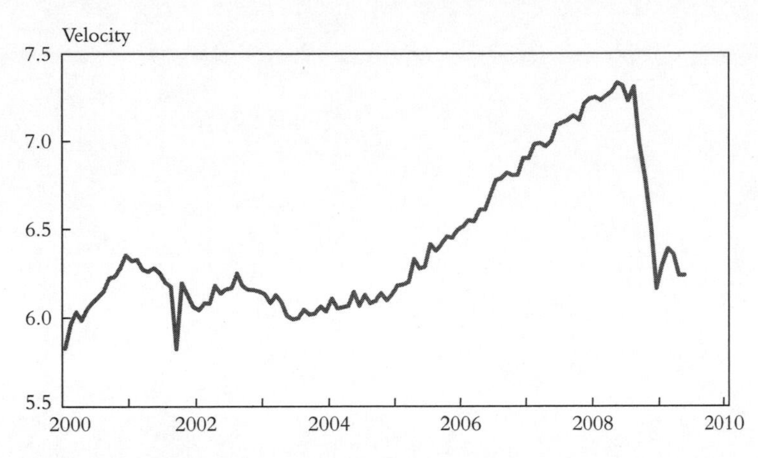

Figure 7.7 Velocity of Money: Personal Consumption Divided by M-1
SOURCE: Bureau of Economic Analysis, Federal Reserve Board

many paid back TARP funds, and the government programs were scaled back considerably. No longer were the markets fearful that a dumb accounting rule would suck the entire system into oblivion.

All of this meant that a more normal economic process could begin. What happened to the economy, the recession that it experienced, was not a normal downturn. It was a panic, a drop in velocity. Because we have not experienced anything like this in our lifetimes, it can be somewhat scary and unpredictable. But since we know what caused it—a series of mistakes by government—we can be reasonably certain that it will end on a better note than the real pessimists fear. With money easy, velocity stabilizing, and mark-to-market finally put behind us, there is finally light at the end of the tunnel.

Moreover, it is reasonable to expect that the economy can trace out a recovery that is as sharp as the recession. And in the second quarter of 2009, a V-shaped recovery, like that traced out in copper prices, the Baltic Freight Index and retail sales was beginning to take shape. For those with eyes to see, the opportunities were plentiful.

Chapter 8

It's Not as Bad as You Think

Satchel Paige is credited with saying, "It's not what you don't know that hurts you, it's what you know that just ain't so." This, I think, is a perfect explanation of the current economic environment. Conventional wisdom argues that an unfathomably complex and interconnected financial system, driven by greed and ambition, was allowed to froth to a peak unchecked by government guardians. And, like a house of cards, once one support was removed, it came crashing down.

One of the most important things an economist does is to tell a story. And this story seems so plausible, so commonsensical. But this story is also wrong. It "ain't so," as Satchel Paige would say. And if investors believe they know a truth that just ain't so, they will make mistakes.

For example, investors continue to hold tremendous levels of cash because they have bought into the belief that the economy will suffer for years to come. Part of this pessimism is driven by serious doubts over capitalism itself, but part is also driven by the underlying view that the economy will grow more slowly in the years ahead. Investors who moved to cash missed a 50+ percent run in the stock market from mid-March to mid-September. And that can't be made up. Moreover, many just won't get into the market now because they expect stock prices will go back down.

These are all big mistakes from my point of view, and they are happening because the conventional wisdom is telling a false story. This book tells a different story, one that is much more optimistic and hopeful. And one that is more in line with history. This book's story goes like this:

- Government was pushing homeownership for decades. Housing was the least taxed, most subsidized investment any consumer could make.
- The Fed cut rates to 1 percent, creating a mirage in the early 2000s. This encouraged excess borrowing by home buyers, excess lending by banks and mortgage brokers, and excess leverage by investment banks.
- This potent brew (90 percent of the blame goes to government, 10 percent goes to the banking system) led to the bubble in housing.
- The Fed lifted rates in 2005 and 2006 and the bubble burst.
- The bursting housing bubble did not need to cause a recession, but mark-to-market accounting acted like an accelerant. It created a vicious downward spiral of financial problems.
- The government, in an attempt to work around the accounting rule and not change it, attempted multiple and costly ad hoc approaches to fix the economy that did not work. The end result was a panic—a massive drop in the velocity of money—the first in 100 years.
- The pessimists were right—a recession occurred—but they were right for the wrong reasons. It did not happen as they said it would. And the recession is ending much more quickly than they said it would. Capitalism is not broken, nor was it the cause of this calamity.

- This was government failure, not market failure.
- Now, easy Fed policy, changes in mark-to-market accounting rules, and an end to the panic have turned the economy and market around.
- A V-shaped recovery is unfolding, not a long, slow slog.
- Capitalism is not as fragile, nor as susceptible to booms and busts, as people fear.

Yes, there are challenges, and yes there is plenty of pain to go around. But the story told here is different, more hopeful, and less deferential to government, than the conventional wisdom. If you believe the story of this book, you will not climb into a hole and become overly concerned about the future. You will not mistrust capitalism or capitalists. And you will worry more about government overstepping its bounds and less about markets.

As for conventional wisdom, Nouriel Roubini may not be its father, but he certainly has been outspoken. Here are a few short excerpts from a column on Forbes.com, titled "The United States of Ponzi," where Roubini comments on the meaning of Bernie Madoff and what he symbolized for the economy:

> Americans lived in a "Made-off" and Ponzi bubble economy for a decade or even longer. Madoff is the mirror of the American economy and of its over-leveraged agents: a house of cards of leverage over leverage by households, financial firms and corporations that has now collapsed in a heap.
>
> When you put zero down on your home, and you thus have no equity in your home, your leverage is literally infinite and you are playing a Ponzi game.
>
> And the bank that lent you, with zero down, a NINJA (no income, no jobs and assets) liar loan that was interest-only for a while, with negative amortization and an initial teaser rate, was also playing a Ponzi game.
>
> And private equity firms that did over a $1 trillion of leveraged buyouts (LBOs) in the past few years with a debt-to-earnings ratio of 10 or above were also Ponzi firms playing a Ponzi game.

> A government that will issue trillions of dollars of new debt to pay for this severe recession and socialize private losses may risk becoming a Ponzi government if—in the medium term—it does not return to fiscal discipline and debt sustainability.[1]

The array of commentators who have propelled the conventional wisdom is breathtaking. Here are some comments that sound a great deal like Roubini's, by David Brooks, a *New York Times* columnist:

> For about a generation, the U.S. surfed on a growing wave of debt. The ratio of debt-to-personal-disposable income was 55 percent in 1960. Since then, it has more than doubled, reaching 133 percent in 2007. Total credit market debt—throwing in corporate, financial and other borrowing—has risen apace, surging from 143 percent of G.D.P. in 1951 to 350 percent of G.D.P. last year.
>
> Charts that mark these trends are truly horrifying. There is a steady level of debt through most of the 20th century, until the mid-1980s. Then there is a steep accelerating rise to today's epic levels.
>
> This rise in debt fueled a consumption binge. Consumption as a share of G.D.P. stood at around 62 percent in the mid-1960s, and rose to about 73 percent by 2008. The baby boomers enjoyed an incredible spending binge. Meanwhile the Chinese, Japanese, and European economies became reliant on the overextended U.S. consumer. It couldn't last.
>
> The leverage wave crashed last fall. Facing the possibility of systemic collapse, the government stepped in and replaced private borrowing with public borrowing. The Federal Reserve printed money at incredible rates, and federal spending ballooned. In 2007, the federal deficit was 1.2 percent of G.D.P. Two years later, it's at 13 percent.[2]

Brooks is considered a conservative, but as we saw in Chapter 5, he seems willing to believe that consumers and businesses are irrational and prone to behavior that is destabilizing. In this view, simple "rules of the road" are not enough. Consumers and financial institutions need to be controlled so they don't make bad decisions that threaten the entire system.

This doom and gloom sprouts new roots and branches every day. It argues that debt will contract and savings will increase, which will slow growth and boost unemployment. Some argue that unemployment alone is enough to drag the economy down. And if that weren't enough, there is fear that new government programs will undermine growth and do damage to the economy.

Arguments like these tend to hit home. They sound plausible, and they fit many people's preconceived notions. After all, we don't believe our own decisions are bad, but if other people's bad decisions can affect us, then this makes us kites in the wind, blown around by things we can do nothing about. This undermines our faith in the system and other people. It makes us want to control other people's behavior, which is the antithesis of conservatism. Fortunately, many of these fears are overstated and misplaced. In the following pages, we will go through them one by one.

Consumer Spending

The data do show that consumption has risen as a share of gross domestic product (GDP) over the past 50 years. To be exact, consumption was 63.9 percent of GDP in late 1960, before falling to 60.6 percent in early 1967. Since then, as can be seen in Figure 8.1, consumption has climbed. It stabilized briefly at about 66 percent of GDP in the late 1980s, and then accelerated again to slightly above 70 percent in the late 1990s and early 2000s. As of the first quarter of 2009, consumption was 70.7 percent of GDP.

But before you jump on the "Americans have become unhinged and spent like drunken sailors" bandwagon, let's take a closer look at the data. Consumers spent 4.6 percent of GDP in the first quarter of 1967 on medical care, but increased this to 13.6 percent of GDP by the first quarter of 2009. This spending includes Medicare and Medicaid reimbursements to hospitals and doctors, which government statisticians count as consumption.

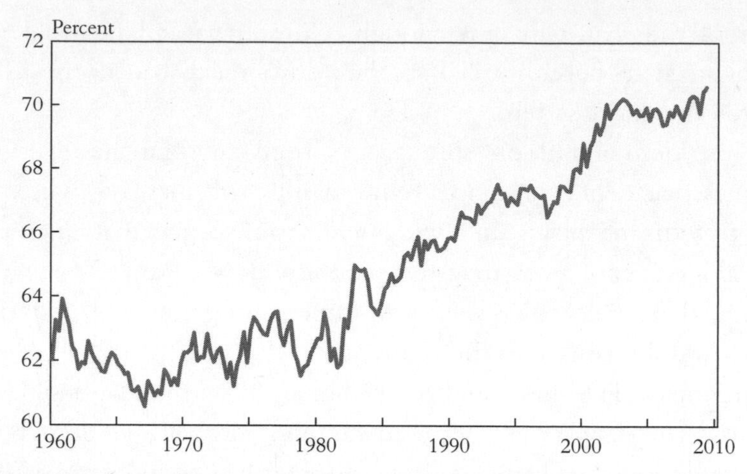

Figure 8.1 Consumption as a Share of Nominal GDP
SOURCE: Bureau of Economic Analysis

Doing the math shows that spending on medical care accounted for 89 percent of the increase in consumption's share of GDP. During those same years private spending on education also increased faster than consumption as a whole, from about 0.8 percent to 1.5 percent of GDP in the past 50 years. This means that 7 percent of the increase in consumption share is accounted for by education. In total, medical care and education accounted for 96 percent of the increase in the consumption share of GDP.

Counting spending on education and medical care as consumption is an interesting concept. We could just as easily count them as investment. After all, spending on these categories lasts a lifetime, literally. Clearly, consumers did not go nuts spending on more material things.

In addition, big-box stores, like Home Depot, Lowe's, Office Depot, and Staples, came into existence in the 1980s, at the exact same time America became much more entrepreneurial. With millions of small businesses opening up their doors, and with their shopping like normal consumers, the government became unable to keep track of business versus consumer spending.

If you buy a computer for your home, but you use it to transact business on eBay, was your spending consumer spending or business spending? The box stores have no idea. They never ask you, so how can the government differentiate? They do try, by assigning a percentage of sales to business investment, but it is highly probable that they are off by a country mile. In America these days, life is very often a combination of business and personal activities all mixed together. This causes consumer spending to be overstated as well because some consumer spending is actually business spending, which should be counted as investment.

Finally, consumer spending is overstated relative to GDP because more and more people are retiring. As we spend our retirement savings and no longer work, we do not add to GDP (which measures production). Bill Gates and Warren Buffett will give away billions in the years ahead to be spent on the poor or on other charitable causes. Even after they are dead, the spending of their foundations will, by definition, boost consumption as a share of GDP.

In other words, what Brooks defines as one of the major problems of our society—overspending—may not exist at all. This is one problem that comes from noneconomists discussing economics. They don't always think things through from the beginning to the end, and they clearly don't understand the vagaries of economic data and its calculation.

Debt

The other area of the economy that is worrisome to the pessimistic set, as well as Brooks and Roubini, is debt. In this arena, we cannot forget that anecdotal information backs up a view of overindebted consumers. We have all heard heartfelt stories about credit card bills, adjustable-rate mortgages, and car loans that have buried people under an avalanche of debt payments. Foreclosures and mortgage delinquencies have been rising rapidly, as have late payments on credit cards.

There are three ways to look at debt burdens. We can look at total debt relative to income, total debt relative to assets, or debt service payments relative to income. The second two measures are much better measures because people can borrow against assets, regardless of income. The key is not what the debt/income ratio is, but whether debt payments can be handled at current levels of income, or covered by selling assets.

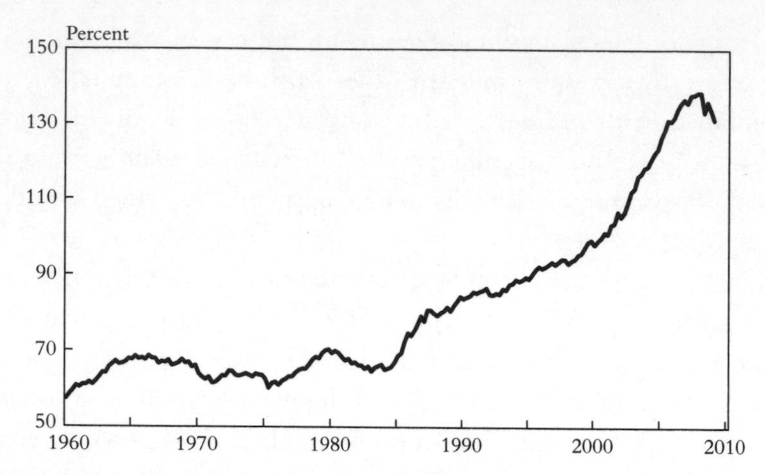

Figure 8.2 Household Debt as a Share of Disposable Personal Income
SOURCE: Bureau of Economic Analysis, Federal Reserve Board

Figure 8.2 presents the conventional wisdom picture, what Brooks calls "horrifying." The chart shows household debt as a share of disposable (after-tax) personal income. The ratio increased from about 60 percent in 1960 to roughly 135 percent in 2007.

However, this data is misleading. Think about the economy of our ancestors, who lived in an environment of subsistence—they ate what they grew or killed. There was virtually no saving—no accumulated assets. Debt was impossible to accumulate because there was nothing to borrow, so the debt-to-income ratio was zero. Eventually, people became more successful and entrepreneurs created surplus. Only then, when people created assets and inventories, could debt be accumulated. Debt requires assets, because if everyone is living hand-to-mouth there is nothing to share, to lend, or to borrow.

Each and every year that people produced more than they consumed, savings grew. At first, accumulated asset levels were less than income, but as success multiplied, the level of assets built up by society (its savings) became greater than annual income. And some of those assets, like housing, had very long lives. And because assets can support debt, the greater the pool of assets, the greater the levels of debt a society can support.

But we must be careful in how we measure the burden of that debt. Here is an example. Let's say someone with no other sources of income owns a rental house worth $200,000, but has a $50,000 mortgage on the property. The mortgage rate is 6 percent, which comes to $3,000 in interest costs per year. The house rents for $1,000 per month—or $12,000 per year. For this person, the debt-to-income ratio is a scary 417 percent ($50,000/$12,000). But the debt service burden ($3,000/$12,000) and the debt-to-asset ratio ($50,000/$200,000) are just 25 percent. In other words, the debt-to-income ratio exaggerates the burden of the debt.

As any economy becomes more successful, as people save and store up assets, sustainable levels of debt will rise. The level of debt to income does not prove that a society is overleveraged. As can be seen in Figure 8.3, households had liabilities that equaled roughly 10 percent of assets in 1960.

Forty-seven years later, in the middle of 2007, liabilities were 18 percent of assets. Still, the average household held assets worth more than five times their debt. In the first quarter of 2009, debt increased to 21.6 percent of assets, but then fell to 20.9 percent in the second quarter. The surge was due to a drop in the value of assets as home prices and equity values fell, not an increase in liabilities. Now that asset values are rising again the ratio is falling.

A much better measure of the burden of debt is what share of our income must be devoted to carrying that debt. The Federal Reserve

Figure 8.3 Household Liabilities as a Share of Assets
SOURCE: Federal Reserve Board

has been calculating data on this measure since 1980. In that year, payments required to support mortgages, consumer debt, rent, automobile lease payments, homeowner's insurance, property taxes—what is called total financial obligations—were 15.8 percent of income.

Financial obligations rose to 17.6 percent of income in 1987, fell back to 16.3 percent in 1993, and then peaked at 19.3 percent of income in 2007. In the first quarter of 2009, with interest rates very low, the ratio had fallen to 18.5 percent of income, which was roughly 1 percentage point above the average during the boom years of 1995 to 1999. (See Figure 8.4.) At these levels, the average debt burden on most people has not reached the "horrifying" levels suggested by debt-to-income ratios.

While some people will get into trouble with debt, most will not. As of the fourth quarter of 2008, 93 percent of prime loans were still paying on time. Yes, a record 11.2 percent of all mortgages were either in foreclosure (3.3 percent) or at least one payment behind (7.9 percent), with 48 percent of adjustable-rate subprime loans delinquent. Many of these numbers are historic highs, but it is important to realize that 55 percent of all mortgage foreclosures were in just five states—Arizona, California, Florida, Michigan, and Nevada. Clearly, this increase in problem mortgages is mostly due to the lending bubble of 2004–2007, but recession and job loss have also added to the total. With

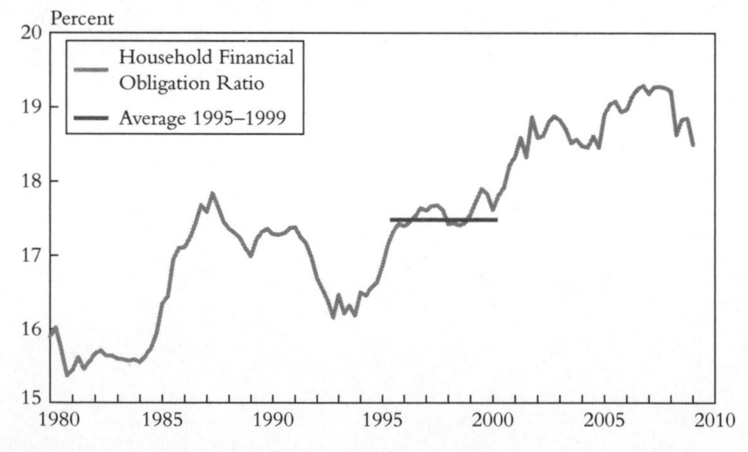

Figure 8.4 Household Financial Obligation Ratio
SOURCE: Federal Reserve Board

housing and the economy stabilizing, and these problems already priced into the market, the worst is behind us. In fact, falling home prices and low interest rates have made homes more affordable. Housing is already picking up again.

There is no doubt that in a very bad economy, or one with soaring interest rates, debt levels could become the whale that breaks the boat apart and drags it into the dark depths. But pessimists have been forecasting such a scenario for more than 40 years. During that time, when the economy was humming along, most people ignored the prognostications. In the past four decades, interest rates have gone up and down and the economy has experienced multiple recessions. Yet wealth continued to grow and living standards continued to rise. Capitalism, as we have repeated many times, is more resilient than assumed by the pessimists.

Growth, Debt, and China

Clearly, many believe that debt has fueled a false and unsustainable increase in economic activity. But this looks at only one side of the coin. Debt and leverage do not cause economic growth any more or less than savings do. What is true for one person, or one entity, is not true for the economy as a whole.

When one person spends more than he earns in a period of time, he must find someone else who will spend less than he earns over that same period of time. Every borrower must be backed up by a saver. Debt is the exchange of present goods against future goods. Debt itself cannot increase consumption today because for every person accelerating his purchases, there must be another person putting those purchases off.

Nonetheless, many analysts insist that the United States used its housing stock like an ATM, taking cash out and boosting GDP growth. But what is possible for one person is not possible for the economy as a whole. If I have a $300,000 house and a $100,000 mortgage, and I open a $50,000 line of credit against the house with a bank, then the bank must have $50,000 in deposits to fund the loan.

Without the deposit, or without borrowing from someone else, the bank cannot make the loan. In other words, the bank must find someone willing to spend less than they earn and lend their "savings" to the bank in order to make a loan. Accountants sometimes know more about economics than economists do, and in this case they would say there must be a credit for every debit. There must be a saver for every borrower.

I can spend $50,000 more than I earn today, but this means that someone else must decide not to spend $50,000. And when I borrow money, I must pay it back. At that point, I spend less than I earn, and the person who lent me the money can now use it to make purchases.

But what if foreigners are doing the saving? China, for instance, holds roughly $800 billion of U.S. Treasury bonds. No matter how many times you hear this argument, it doesn't change the dynamic at all. The only difference between China and any other saver is that they are a foreign country. Eventually, China must spend that money. The dollar system is a closed system. Money does not leak or disappear. Some worry that China will dump its dollars, so let's look at what happens.

China starts by selling its $800 billion in Treasury bonds—all at once. If China did this, it would probably shock the world, and Treasury yields would soar. How high, who knows, but let's assume the 10-year Treasury yield goes to 10 percent. China gets U.S. dollars in return for its sales, but it doesn't want those dollars, so it trades them to a Swiss bank for euros. China is now out of dollars, which is exactly what they wanted. But the Swiss bank has the $800 billion. What does it do with them?

Well, how about buying those 10-year Treasury bonds at 10 percent? If it did so, it would drive the price up and the yield down, right back to where it was before this shell game started. The dollars did not disappear, they just moved around. If you followed this set of transactions, then you know that China would never do this, because it would take a huge loss on the trade. China does not hold our debt because it wants to be nice to us; it holds our debt because it is the best choice available.

When a Chinese producer sells goods to Wal-Mart for dollars it then must give those dollars to the government in exchange for renminbi

(RMB), its local currency. Then the producer has the RMB and the central bank has dollars, which it uses to back its circulating currency.

Chinese currency does not circulate in the world financial system, so that currency is good only within China's borders. If RMB could be used outside of China, or if the Chinese central bank were to allow its people to convert local currency back into dollars, the trade balance might change significantly, with more Chinese buying goods and services from the United States.

But, for now, China has decided to keep its currency untradeable, while it invests its dollar reserves in U.S. assets. Treasury debt is the largest holding, but China is also investing directly into U.S. businesses. For example, in 2007, China invested $3 billion directly in Blackstone, a major U.S. private-equity firm. It has made other investments as well.

As long as China is comfortable making investments in the United States, then this situation will persist. But no matter what China decides to do, those dollars must be spent in the United States to purchase U.S. assets or U.S. goods and services. They cannot be spent or invested anywhere else.

Some say that large holdings of U.S. assets by foreign governments created an "ocean of money"—what Fed Chairman Ben Bernanke called a "global savings glut"—which drove down long-term interest rates and fueled a binge of borrowing.

But let's think this through. Imagine that we never bought anything from China at all, and instead Americans saved all this money themselves. The U.S. trade deficit would be much lower, and there would still be an "ocean of savings," but it would be held by Americans. Then, with all this savings and very low interest rates, there still would have been a housing boom.

Who holds the resources—whether it is American savers or Chinese savers—does not matter; the money still has to be invested. And dollars must be invested in dollar assets, they can't be invested anywhere else. In other words, no matter where the money is sent or how it is spent or saved, it still exists. The dollar system is a closed system; there is no leakage or spillage.

Deleveraging

One other fear is that deleveraging will hold the United States back in the years ahead and that no solid recovery can take place until this process is complete. The idea here is that all that borrowing we saw in Figure 8.2 drove up consumption, and now that people will be more rational and this leverage (borrowing) will decline, the economy will slow.

But this is one of the most frequent mistakes in macroeconomics—confusing debt expansion with money creation. Contrary to popular belief, individual banks and credit card companies do not create new money. They can provide money to their customers only if they borrow it from someone else first.

The "banking system" can multiply deposits and create money, but not individual banks or credit card companies. In a fractional reserve banking system, the Federal Reserve can inject high-powered money (the monetary base) by buying bonds from a bank. That bank then puts some of that money (say 10 percent) in reserve and lends out the rest. This loan then turns into a deposit at another bank. The second bank puts 10 percent into reserve and makes another loan. It is this process that multiplies the Fed's initial injection of high-powered money.

Some people assume this means that savings themselves are multiplied or that an individual bank can create money. But this is not the case. A dollar of saving can be lent only a single time at any one institution. Only if the Fed injects new money can the system create new money. There must be a debit for every credit, a depositor for every borrower. Money and credit are different.

Remember, the only way one person can spend more than he earns is to have someone else spend less than he earns. Every loan is backed by a dollar of savings. Debt and leverage by themselves do not create money. Therefore, deleveraging does not destroy money or resources.

Think about it this way: Imagine a hedge fund raises $100 million of capital and then borrows $500 million from a bank in order to employ a leveraged investment strategy. The bank does not create $500 million; it lends other people's deposits. In other words, this leverage does not create anything new. It just shifts resources from one place to another—in this case from the depositors to the hedge fund.

Let's now assume the bank calls in its loan. The deleveraging process begins and the hedge fund repays the $500 million to the bank. What, then, does the bank do with this money? It lends it out again, of course. Even if it buys T-bills, it is lending the money to the government. If it holds the funds as excess reserves at the Fed, the Fed then turns around and buys bonds or commercial paper with the money. If the bank buys municipal bonds, it is lending to a state or local government.

No matter what happens—unless the bank converts the balance to hard money and sticks it in a vault where it would earn no interest and not circulate at all—the money goes right back into the system. It does not disappear. Deleveraging does not subtract money from the economy because leverage never created any new money. As a result, deleveraging does not by itself lead to less economic growth.

One argument some analysts make at this point is "What if the hedge fund went broke and could not repay its $500 million?" Or "Don't falling asset values destroy money, and doesn't that hurt economic activity?"

Well, let's think about it. If the hedge fund went broke, the bank would lose $500 million. Presumably, the hedge fund used the $500 million to purchase an investment, and the firm that sold that investment would still have the $500 million. It's a deposit in some other bank. If a house that was purchased for $500,000 falls in value to $350,000, the owner has lost $150,000 on paper. But the person who sold the house to the new owner still has the $500,000. Money does not disappear even though asset values can fall.

None of this can cause the money supply to contract. The only way the economy can experience a contraction in the money supply, or in credit, is if the Federal Reserve removes money from the system or allows bank deposits to contract when banks fail. In the Great Depression, the Federal Reserve made this mistake. Today, however, the Fed is injecting reserves and the Federal Deposit Insurance Corporation (FDIC) is making certain that bank assets are merged into other banks. The money supply is increasing, not contracting, as it did in much of the 1930s.

This does not mean deleveraging has no impact. It definitely affects interest rates. In the early 2000s, when the Fed cut interest rates to 1 percent, this set off an addictive use of leverage. Hedge funds and other special investment vehicles levered up at very low short-term interest rates to buy securitized debt (car loans, credit card debt, mortgages).

To make 30 percent returns at 10:1 leverage, the fund needed 3 percent spreads; at 20:1, a 1.5 percent spread could work; and at 30:1, a spread of just 1 percent would satisfy. As leverage proliferated, lending rates were pulled down sharply, which helped fuel the boom in housing.

The Fed pushed this process along because it held short-term interest rates very low, and even when it was raising rates it broadcast its moves well in advance. As a result, many financial institutions were willing to make highly leveraged loans at very low interest rates, thinking they were taking very little risk. This in turn encouraged more borrowing and more leverage.

But now that this leverage is being unwound, credit spreads have widened. Higher interest rates on corporate debt, car loans, and credit cards are partly the result of having less leverage in the system. This does not mean that there is less money, just less leverage.

Instead of having money concentrated in highly leveraged hedge funds, investment banks, or other investment vehicles, it will be spread out among many more, less leveraged institutions. Those institutions that never levered up to such extreme levels, like community banks, will find themselves more competitive in the auto, small business, and consumer loan markets. The same amount of money will circulate in the system, but leverage will be used much more sparingly, and interest rates charged to borrowers will be higher.

None of this will harm economic growth, and a look at the past 50 years of history can prove it. Back in the 1960s and 1970s—the "good ol' days" of high savings rates and low borrowing—nominal GDP was growing much faster than it has in the past 30 years. Figure 8.5 shows the same debt-to-income ratio we saw in Figure 8.2. This time

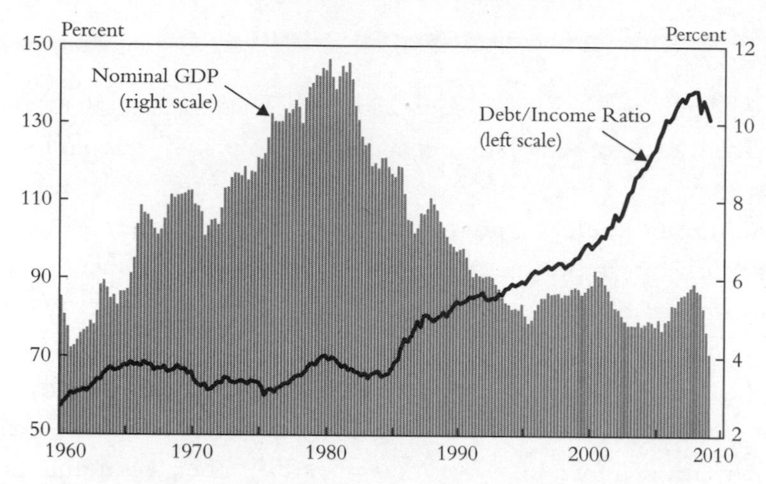

Figure 8.5 Five-Year Annualized Percent Change in Nominal GDP versus Household Debt/Income Ratio
SOURCE: Bureau of Economic Analysis, Federal Reserve Board

we are juxtaposing the five-year average nominal GDP growth rate against it.

In the 1970s, when household debt averaged roughly 60 percent of disposable personal income, nominal GDP grew at an average pace of 10 percent. But between 1995 and 2005, when consumer debt averaged over 100 percent of income, nominal GDP averaged only 5.5 percent growth. In other words, no matter how many times you hear that leverage increases economic activity, and no matter how commonsensical it sounds, it is just not true.

And before you argue that this comparison uses nominal GDP and not real GDP, think about it for a second. Real GDP is inflation adjusted. When was the last time you spent an inflation-adjusted dollar? You haven't, you never have, you spend nominal dollars. But for the sake of this argument, real GDP averaged 4.3 percent annual growth in the 1960s, 3.3 percent in the 1970s, 3.1 percent in the 1980s, 3.2 percent in the 1990s, and 2.0 percent in the past 10 years. There is no evidence whatsoever that leverage and borrowing increase economic activity—real or nominal.

Unemployment

Many argue that the economy cannot improve as long as the unemployment rate is high. The theory here is simple. As people lose their jobs, they spend less, which creates more job losses, which causes less spending, and the cycle goes round and round and there is little hope that much can improve anytime soon. But this is a circular argument. The cycle of cause and effect never ends. Here is a hint: When you hear a circular story in economics, something is wrong.

Let's think about this process in the opposite fashion, by asking how a recession could ever begin? If more jobs cause more spending, which creates more jobs and more spending, then economic growth should never stop. This idea of a perpetual motion machine between jobs and spending cannot possibly exist. If it did, both recessions and recoveries would never end.

But we know this is not the case. Recessions and recoveries come and go. There must be something beyond unemployment that drives this process. History is quite clear: It is monetary policy that has caused just about every business cycle since 1913. That was the year the Fed was first begun. The Fed tightens too much and the economy turns down. Then the Fed eases policy and the economy picks back up.

Such an approach even worked in the 1970s when high taxes, regulation, and spending should have held back growth and offset monetary policy. But in 1972–1974, tight Fed policy caused a sharp decline in economic activity and the stock market crashed—a really serious bear market. The Fed then reversed course and the economy turned up.

The unemployment rate rose from 4.6 percent in October 1973 to 7.2 percent in December 1974. Then it went up again to 9 percent by May 1975. But the stock market bottomed in December 1974, with the S&P 500 up 34 percent between then and May, when the unemployment rate finally peaked. At the same time, inflation-adjusted consumer spending grew a rapid 3.5 percent annual rate in the first quarter of 1975 and 6.7 percent in the second quarter. All of this happened even though the unemployment rate was still rising.

Job losses are not fun, and with the unemployment rate near 10 percent in 2009, it is hard to convince anyone that anything is good about the economy. But after the unemployment rate hit 10.7 percent in the fourth quarter of 1982, real GDP grew 7.5 percent at an annual rate in the first three quarters of 1983. While it is hard to imagine that the U.S. economy will grow this fast in the year ahead, the idea that it can't grow at all because unemployment is high just doesn't hold water. The unemployment rate is often the last piece of economic data to show an improvement in economic activity.

When we look back, much like the 1970s, the recession will probably have ended sometime in May or June 2009 even though the unemployment rate was still rising. Just like 1975–1976, those who watch unemployment will be late to the party. It is only a matter of time before the job market improves, but by then the stock market will have already risen substantially.

Savings Rates

A rebound in employment may not be enough to turn pessimists into optimists. Even if the unemployment rate begins to fall, many worry that consumers will start to save more and spend less (even though, earlier, they were worried that consumers weren't saving enough). As David Brooks frets, a ". . . country that has become accustomed to reasonably fast growth and frothy affluence will probably have to adjust to slower growth and less retail fizz."[3]

Wow, really? The only way to keep the economy going strong is to keep borrowing and spending money like drunken sailors? Is there any evidence of this, anywhere? What about countries that save a lot. How are they doing?

"The saving rate in China is the highest of any major country . . . , [and] . . . the saving rate in the United States is the lowest of any major country . . . " says Robert Shiller, economics professor at Yale University. He then adds, "Differences in saving rates matter a lot, and must be a major reason that China's annual economic growth rate is now a full six percentage points higher than in the U.S."[4]

Oops. Which is it? Do savings increase economic growth or slow economic growth? The answer is: We don't know, partly because we can't measure savings very well. Savings rates themselves are a terrible measure of the true resources of any economy. People, ideas, and entrepreneurship are where the real value of an economy is found. Jeff Bezos and his little venture called Amazon is a creator of wealth and jobs. Apple's iPhone creates value and growth and employment. The savings rate tells us nothing about this. Entrepreneurship is the real wealth creator.

The reason that China is growing faster than the United States is not because it saves more; it's because it has moved toward a free-market economy while leapfrogging generations of technological advances. What took the United States decades to invent and proliferate, China can put to use in a matter of years. Skip the copper phone lines and go straight to cellular phones. Now that's a recipe for rapid growth.

The Economy Will Recover

The United States can't roll out cellular phones all over again, so we may not grow as fast as China as it benefits from technological advances that it borrows from other countries. But does that mean that the United States is destined to grow more slowly than it has in the past? "Not at all" is the appropriate answer.

During every recession of the past 40 years or so, there has been a very vocal contingent of voices suggesting that "this time we pushed it too far." As has been noted in earlier chapters, there seems to be a ready-made audience that thinks the wealth created in the United States is "false" and "unsustainable." It seems that the more success America has, the greater the doubts are that it can, or will, continue.

Part of this is political because every crisis can be turned to someone's advantage if played right. But, for the most part, this is just human nature. Many of the well-known philosophers—Nietzsche, Freud, Rousseau, Camus, Schopenhauer, and Foucault—were pessimists, not necessarily about the economy, but about human nature and life in a disorderly universe. These philosophers didn't tell people how to think; they were just the first, or the most capable, at putting this side of human nature into words. Some people just can't get used to good things happening.

And as Ludwig von Mises pointed out all the way back in 1956:

> Under capitalism the common man enjoys amenities which in ages gone by were unknown and therefore inaccessible even to the richest people. But, of course, these motorcars, television sets and refrigerators do not make a man happy. In the instant in which he acquires them, he may feel happier than he did before. But as soon as some of his wishes are satisfied, new wishes spring up. Such is human nature.[5]

In other words, it's natural, even for people living better than the kings of yesteryear, to lose faith. The good news is that economic pessimists have been wrong. That's why we are still here. If life expectancy were still 24 years, as it was in 1000 A.D., two-thirds of us would not be here today. If gains in life expectancy had stopped in 1820, at 36 years, one-half of us would not be here. If we had not invented the air conditioner, Congress would still be working only a few months a year because it's just too hot in Washington, D.C. Oh, wait . . . then things would be really, really good. Did pessimists invent the air conditioner?

Seriously, the U.S. economy has recovered from every recession, every panic, and every depression it has ever experienced, partly because of the insatiable appetite people have for bettering their condition. But this well-known fact does not stop the pessimism. As a result, many people worry that the United States is on the cusp of another Great Depression or a repeat of the 1970s.

For investors, especially those who are counting on investment returns for retirement, hearing that we could be headed to another long period of decline or malaise is a nightmare. While I seriously doubt that the United States is in for another Great Depression, even if it were, an investor should realize that in both the 1970s and in the 1930s, in the middle of those terrible decades, the stock markets experienced monster rallies.

The rallies were caused by a very accommodative monetary policy, just like the United States is experiencing right now. While this will eventually boost inflation, the first impact is that the economy and stock market will head significantly higher. The next 12 to 18 months are likely to be boom times for America.

If Congress passes, and President Obama signs into law, climate change legislation, national health care, and a major tax hike, the economy will suffer. However, those events still have not happened, nor will they affect the economy in any dramatic way until at least 2011.

What this means is that the economy has some clear running room for now. Get ready for the V-shaped recovery.

Chapter 9

It's Boom Time Again

I was driving in downtown Chicago not long ago, heading for the Drake Hotel, and I was a little lost. I had forgotten which direction the one-way street in front of the Drake moved. With just a few blocks to go, I used my cell phone to call a friend at his desk. In about 60 seconds, he had pulled up an online map, and told me that Walton Place went east to west.

Missing a one-way street in a large city during rush hour can be a huge mistake. The good news is that I didn't miss it. Because of my cell phone, my friend's computer, the Internet, and Google maps, I saved at least a few minutes, possibly 15, and I got to talk to my friend. I could have saved even more time if I had a global positioning system in my car.

In our big world, this is a little, little thing. But these little things start adding up when you consider the total number of people who can now regularly make use of small, time-saving devices. Worldwide, at least 4 billion cell phones are in use today. And every year, hundreds of millions more are added to the network. Access to the Internet is expanding daily, search engines are getting better, communication speeds are getting faster, and handheld devices are getting more powerful.

Multiply the minutes and hours of time savings per day by billions of users, and the benefits of all this technology are massive. They make the gains from railroads, automobiles, airplanes, the telegraph, and copper phone lines look tiny by comparison. The power of technology is not in the big things; it's in the little things. And this is just one area of improving technology.

Health care, energy, transportation, and information technologies are improving rapidly. And with these improving technologies, every sector of the economy, every industry is becoming more productive and less wasteful. Nonfarm productivity—a standard measure of efficiency calculated by the government—has nearly tripled between 1947 and today. This means one man-hour of labor can produce three times what it could produce a little more than 60 years ago.

Karl Marx said that workers would not benefit from this increase in productivity, but he has been proven decisively wrong. Not only has worker compensation, adjusted for inflation, risen just as fast as productivity in the past 60 years, but the prices of goods and services have fallen relative to income.

In 1947, Americans spent 32.6 percent of all their consumption dollars on food and 11.7 percent on clothing and shoes. In 2009, food takes up just 13.8 percent, while clothing and shoes represent just 3.7 percent of total consumption. In 1960, 7.3 percent of the American consumer's budget was spent on energy (gas, electricity, heating, and air conditioning). Today, even with so-called high energy prices, it's just 5.1 percent.

The average American, at least in terms of material things, lives three times better than his or her grandparents did in the 1940s. And because of advances in health care and better living conditions, an American male born today has a life expectancy 10 years longer than if he had been born in 1950 (female life expectancy has increased by 13 years).

It is true that the top 1 percent of income earners have seen massive gains in income that have surpassed those of the median income earner. And it is also true that some people measure themselves versus other people. But the fact that the median income earner has not experienced the same increase in earnings as those athletes who play left tackle in the National Football League does not mean that their incomes or living standards fell. Despite some relative shifts in income, the average worker is significantly better off today than 10, 20, 30, 40, or 50 years ago.

Just as importantly, the benefits of growth and wealth creation are spreading around the world. In the past two decades, in China and India alone, hundreds of millions of people have been lifted out of poverty. Freedom—and its attendant benefits, such as economic growth—has spread, even to the former communist countries of eastern Europe. Global trade has increased dramatically, and until the recent crisis, worldwide real economic growth had been setting records.

The idea that all of this has now come to a screeching halt because of a few hundred billion dollars of bad mortgage loans is actually quite absurd. As we have seen, bureaucratic bungling turned what was a serious financial market problem into a run on the global banking system. If you really want to be mad, be mad at the governments that did not suspend mark-to-market accounting right away.

As I have explained, it was this accounting rule that led to the death of some stalwart, old-line financial firms. It was also a key cause of the panic by consumers and businesses in late 2008. Now that the prices of toxic securities have fallen to rock-bottom levels, while mark-to-market accounting rules have been relaxed, the danger from further write-downs is past. The system is healing.

Sunk costs just don't impact a capitalist system. When firms fail and financial losses are booked, and when prices hit bottom, it's all water under the bridge. There is no reason to look back. This does not mean that financial markets will snap back immediately and do exactly what they did before. There will definitely be a psychological impact. After you touch a hot stove, you are more careful the next time. But the pain from burning your fingers does not stop you from cooking.

And that's what the economy is about to do—start cooking with three main ingredients: easy money, the end of panic, and some relief from mark-to-market accounting. But the most important of these, the one that will drive the economy inexorably upward in the next 12 to 24 months, is the fact that the Fed has become so accommodative. The U.S. economy is floating on a sea of liquidity.

Don't Fight the Fed

The Federal Reserve is the only entity in the U.S. that can write a check with no money in a bank account and not worry about it bouncing. The Fed can print its own money. To be more precise, the Fed can create money out of thin air by crediting it to the account of any banking entity that it has a relationship with.

The Fed has to obey accounting rules. Its assets must equal its liabilities, which means that it can increase its assets by buying Treasury bonds or mortgage-backed securities from a bank as long as it pays for those bonds by issuing dollars. The dollars are a liability of the Fed, and the Fed can create as many dollars as it wants. And when the Fed prints (or creates) more money (dollars), these dollars are then spent, and they turn into economic activity.

Bob Genetski, former chief economist at Chicago's Harris Bank, tells a story about "Sam the Counterfeiter" to explain how money works. You see, Sam had perfect $100 plates. He set up a printing press in his mother's basement and gave $100 bills to his mother and his girlfriend and kept some for himself.

His mother went furniture shopping and his girlfriend started buying new clothes, while Sam hung out at the bar buying drinks for everyone and placing bets with his bookie. The furniture store and the dress shop are booming, so they buy inventory and hire more workers. The bar is packed and it buys a new big-screen television. The bookie acquires a computer to keep track of all the bets. Sam's town is booming.

Then the FBI swoops in and takes away Sam, his $100 plates, and every $100 bill they can find. The furniture store goes bankrupt, the dress shop has a sidewalk sale and trims its staff, the bar raffles off the TV, and the bookie leaves the small town for the big city. The town goes bust. Money is a very powerful force that drives short-term swings in the economy (what economists call cyclical swings).

If the Fed prints just enough money to accommodate productivity improvements, then there is no inflation. Using the natural rate model from Chapter 5, if the Fed holds short-term rates near the natural rate, then it means that it is adding just the right amount of money to "pay for" all the new goods and services that are created. In other words, money growth is equal to economic growth, which means prices stay stable.

If the Fed adds more money to the system than it needs, this drives interest rates below the natural rate, increases economic growth, and eventually creates inflation. If the Fed adds less money than the system demands, this drives interest rates above the natural rate, slows economic growth, and eventually lowers inflation.

As of midyear 2009, the Fed was holding the federal funds rate well below the natural rate. The funds rate was 0.13 percent, while the two-year annualized rate of change in nominal GDP was 0.5 percent. If we exclude housing, which was clearly weaker than the rest of the economy, the two-year annualized rate of change was 1.7 percent. Either way, the Fed was following an accommodative monetary policy, which meant the Fed was adding excess money to the economy. This money, just like Sam's crisp new $100 bills, is guaranteed to drive economic activity in an upward arc. It will also lift commodity prices and inflation.

1975–1976 Redux?

In 1972, nominal GDP was growing at an average annual rate of about 9 percent, but the Fed started the year with a federal funds rate of just 3.5 percent. In other words, the Fed was super easy. Because inflation was accelerating, the Fed started tightening monetary policy, eventually lifting the funds rate to 12.9 percent in July 1974—well above GDP growth, which was then 10 percent. This meant that the Fed had become very tight. See Figures 5.1 and 5.2.

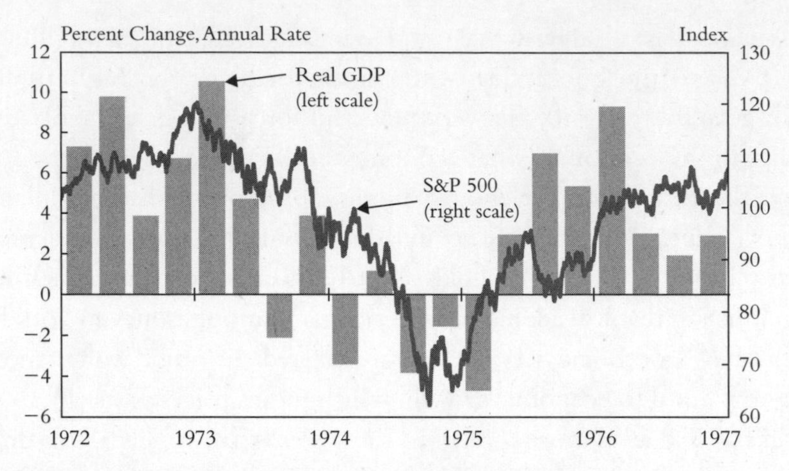

Figure 9.1 Real GDP Growth Rate versus S&P 500 (1972–1977)
SOURCE: Bureau of Economic Analysis, Standard and Poor's

As a result of this tight monetary policy, and the near quadrupling of short-term interest rates, the U.S. economy sunk into a very nasty recession. Figure 9.1 shows the annualized changes in real gross domestic product (GDP) on a quarterly basis from 1972 to 1977. The NBER says the recession did not start until November 1973, but the first decline in real GDP was in the third quarter.

From that point, the economy contracted in five out of the next seven quarters, one of the longest and most severe post–World II recessions. The stock market also cracked, with the S&P 500 stock index falling from 118.05 in December 1972 to 63.54 in December 1974. This 48 percent decline in stock prices was one of the worst bear markets in history. It was relentless.

But then the Fed reversed course, not by making a gentle U-turn, but by engaging in a Bob Bondurant driving school power slide. The Fed cut the funds rate from 12.9 percent to 5.2 percent in just 10 months. By November 1974, the funds rate was below the GDP growth rate. The stock market bottomed in September 1974, and the S&P 500 was back to 107 by December 1976. The economy also accelerated sharply, with real GDP growing 7.2 percent at an annual rate between June 1975 and March 1976. The power of easy monetary policy was easy to see.

Can It Happen Again?

So the forecasting dilemma is whether this can happen again in 2009–2010. The answer is "of course." However, there is a difference. The Fed never did raise interest rates above nominal GDP in 2007. The Fed was never tight. (See Figures 5.1 and 5.2 in Chapter 5.) The Panic of 2008, as we have seen, was caused by a drop in the velocity of money, not tight money. So when the Fed cut the funds rate from 5.25 percent in mid-2007 to 0.13 percent in December 2008, it went from an easy monetary policy to a super-easy monetary policy.

All that needs to happen is for velocity to stabilize (or increase), which appears to be happening. Then, as the money supply kicks in, the economy will pick up steam as if by magic. That's the way money works. It always has, and it always will.

What is interesting is that at the end of every recession there are those who argue that easy money won't work this time. One of the most common observations is that the Fed is "pushing on a string." In other words, the Fed is helpless because the banking system is messed up, unemployment is rising, debt levels are too high, or many other reasons. But no matter how many times people say this, it never seems to be true. The lesson of history is not to fight the Fed.

Panics End

Maybe the hardest fear for investors to overcome, even optimistic ones, is that something major has changed for the worse. After the crash of 1987, many argued that investors would never come back. The same thing was heard after the dot-com crash of 2000–2002. Not only were investors shell-shocked, but there was fear that the fall in asset prices could lead to less spending, which would lead to less job growth, which would lead to further declines in assets prices.

This leads to a highly scientific observation on my part—dogs bark. You can tell them to stop, and they may for a few minutes, but then they bark again. Banks make loans; they don't make hamburgers. If they don't make loans, then they aren't banks. And people spend—that's what they do, at least if they want to live. They have to have clothes to wear to work, food to sustain them, children to educate, and so on. The idea that a zebra will change its stripes and become a horse is highly unlikely. I suppose it could happen, but it has never happened before. So why would you ever arrange your affairs as if it would happen this time? Sitting in cash, earning 0.2 percent, is a very costly approach if you are wrong, especially when inflation is accelerating.

Panics end—that's what they do. Even the Panic of 1907, which saw a 14.8 percent drop in real GDP in the two years following the 1906 San Francisco earthquake, came to an end. No one knows exactly why the panic started or why it continued to spread, but it did. And in 1907 there was no Fed. The textbooks say that the way to counteract a drop in the velocity of money is to add more money, but in 1907 there was no way to do that. So the United States had to wait it out. Wait until asset prices bottomed and all the bankruptcies had been declared. Once that happened, the market and the economy recovered strongly.

As can be seen in Figure 9.2, the Dow fell 49 percent in 1906–1907, bottomed in November, and then increased by 61 percent in late 1907 and 1908. The second line in the chart is the stock market starting in 2008. I actually hate charts like this. The implication of them is always

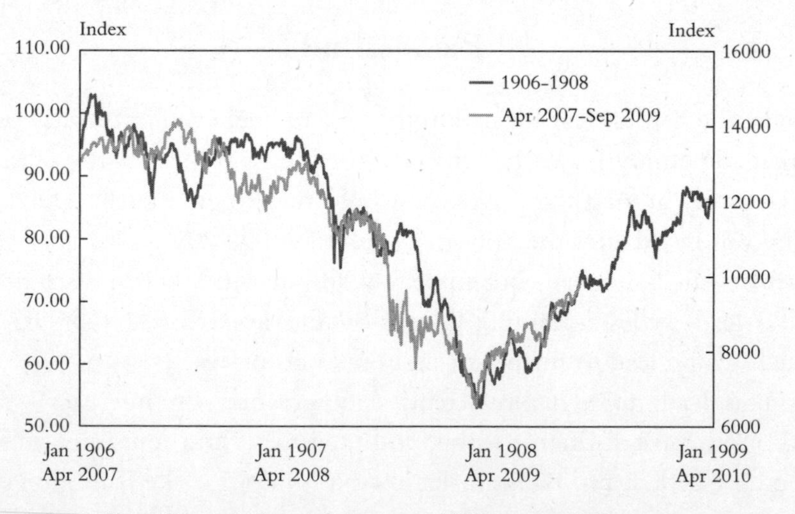

Figure 9.2 Dow Jones Industrial Average, 1907 versus 2008
SOURCE: Ibbotson

that history is repeating itself, but if that happens, it's a coincidence. There is little reason to believe that markets will move the same today as they did 100 years ago. Nonetheless, it is still uplifting to see that the last time a true panic took down the economy, the markets recovered.

It Won't Stay Down Forever

One thing overlooked in the midst of panics is how deeply they cut into the normal markets for things. For instance, as we have seen, car sales have not been keeping up with scrap rates, while housing starts have fallen to one-third the level necessary to keep up with population growth and worn out or destroyed houses.

Another way to look at housing is to look at the pipeline of new homes coming onto the market. In Figure 9.3, the number of new homes under construction and for sale (what are called "spec" homes because they are being built speculatively) fell to 112,000 in July, the lowest level on record going back to 1970. This level is even below the bottom reached in 1982, when population was roughly 30 percent less than today. In other words, builders have become massively risk averse. Eventually, this must change, even if it takes new competitors to sense opportunity and respond.

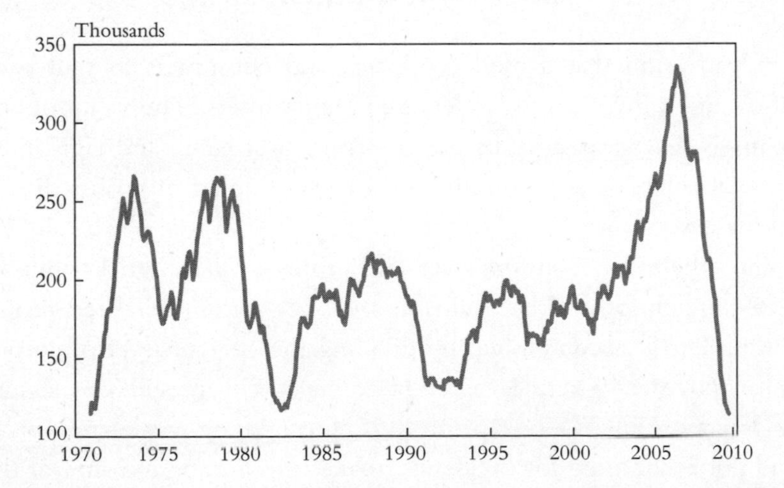

Figure 9.3 New Single-Family Houses: Under Construction and For Sale
SOURCE: Census Bureau

The same thing has happened with retailers and manufacturers. Even though many worried about the economy, the Panic of 2008 and the complete collapse in activity as velocity fell caught them by surprise. They shut down. The data show that inventories at manufacturers, retailers, and wholesalers fell $123 billion in the eight months between July 2008 and April 2009. This is by far the biggest drop in measured history. Nothing else even comes close.

Manufacturing, foreign trade, retail sales, housing, autos, grocery stores, bars and restaurants, transportation, and commodity prices all reflected the drop in velocity during late 2008 and early 2009. Risk aversion became the name of the game. Yes, financing was more difficult to obtain, and non-Treasury interest rates were higher as leverage was unwound, but the real problem is that perceived risks to investing rose sharply.

This led to a pullback in every sector of the economy, to unsustainably low levels. Industrial production has experienced its sharpest declines since the 1973–1974 bear market and recession. But with retail sales and final demand now bouncing back, many producers are finding themselves behind the curve. Shortages are developing. As a result, like 1975–1976, the recovery is already looking like a V.

Undervalued Markets

The risk aversion that caused producers and consumers to pull back has also caused investors to undervalue equity assets. The value of any company is determined by its profit stream over time, and right now the market is paying significantly less for every dollar of profits than it has in the past.

While there are many ways to use profits to value stocks, one of the most straightforward and valuable methods is the capitalized-profits approach. This is accomplished by dividing the current level of corporate profits by the 10-year Treasury bond yield. This provides a measure of the present value of future profits. Of course, using just current profits, and not accounting for dividends, makes this a static measure of the market. In a growing economy, profits and dividends will rise over time.

The best measure of profits is provided by the Bureau of Economic Analysis using data collected by the Internal Revenue Service (IRS). The alternative is individual corporate earnings reports. While both numbers are likely very well documented and mathematically correct, the profits reported to the government are likely more accurate for valuing corporations. If a company actually pays taxes on it, it must be real profits.

Some analysts argue that using the 10-year Treasury yield (the risk-free rate) leads to a potential bias in the model. Corporate bonds trade at a spread over Treasuries because of risk. Therefore, dividing by a lower yield (the Treasury) would put a higher present value on future profits. There are two reasons to ignore this concern. First, because the model uses Treasury yields to discount profits for the entire history of the data (back to 1953), if there is a bias, it is always the same and therefore can be ignored.

Second, because the model uses current earnings, with no accounting for potential future growth, this biases the model in the downward direction. If you expect earnings to continue to grow over time, which is what history suggests they will do, then using current earnings underestimates the value of companies. So, the upward bias from using the Treasury yield is offset by the use of static one-year earnings.

Dividing overall U.S. corporate profits by the 10-year Treasury yield generates an index. Setting the index equal to the S&P 500 at some point in the past and assuming that the market was fairly valued at that point then allows the model to use profits today and interest rates today to compare to that past level.

However, the starting point of the comparison is very important. If the index is anchored during a quarter when stocks were overvalued, then the model will have a bias in that direction and it will overstate the real value of stocks over time. If the index is linked to stocks during a quarter when stocks were undervalued, it will be biased in the opposite direction.

To overcome that issue, the model presented here values the market in the current quarter by comparing it to the model's valuation using *every* quarter back to 1953, and taking an average of the results.

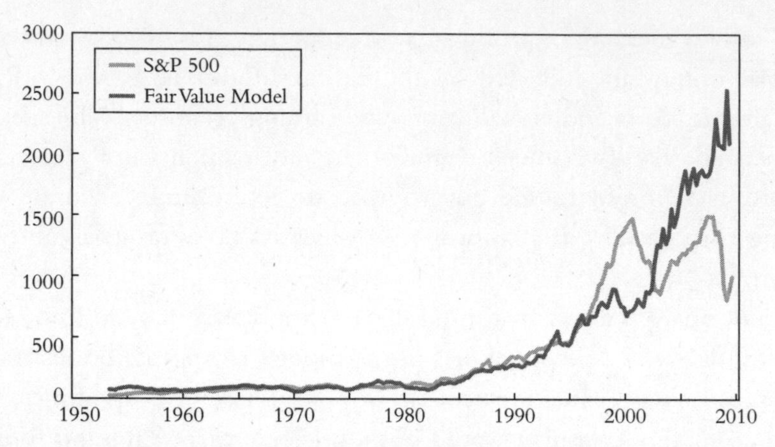

Figure 9.4 Capitalized Profits and Stock Prices
SOURCE: BEA, FRB, Standard & Poor's, and First Trust Portfolios LP

This makes certain that the model is not biased by any starting point. Figure 9.4 shows the actual value of the S&P 500 versus the capitalized profits model for the past 56 years.

As we can see, the market is not often fairly valued. It is typically overvalued or undervalued. And the fact that the model says the market is under- or overvalued does not the mean the market will move up or down. According to the model, stocks were overvalued for most of the 1980s and again in the late 1990s, but moved up anyway.

The model also shows that the S&P 500 has been undervalued since 2002, yet stocks have had a very difficult time in the past seven years. The good news is that when the market is undervalued, the long-term risks from purchasing stocks are low. When we can buy a dollar of future profits for less than it has cost in the past to buy a dollar of future profits, it's a good long-term investment.

Yes, profits have come down. And yes, some people worry that profits will fall further. And yes, many analysts worry about the direction of government policy (as they should). But the market has all of this priced in already. In other words, when the model says the market is so significantly undervalued, the potential for a further decline in equity prices is smaller than the potential for an increase in equity prices.

One of the keys for believing this is the health of the economy. If it grows in the next few years and profits rise, then the stock market will become even more undervalued and it will be very difficult for this not to be accounted for by market prices. If investors refuse to push stock prices higher, then management will buy back stock, companies will be taken private, and mergers and acquisitions will increase. This, in turn, will lift stock prices.

This is one of the reasons that demographic models will be wrong when it comes to stock prices. A few analysts argue that, as baby boomers wind down their working careers and no longer accumulate stock, the demand for U.S. equities will fall and this will pull prices down. But stocks are valued on their earnings, their cash flow, not on the demand for their stock. If the market won't value a company at a high enough price, there are multiple ways for management to extract that value.

Productivity and Profits

If corporate profits are the mother's milk of economic growth, productivity is the baby. Without productivity growth, there would be no profits. And without profits, entrepreneurs would never look for ways to produce goods and services for less than consumers are willing to pay.

Productivity growth is the only way that living standards are increased over time. If the world had never become more efficient at producing things, our lives would be little different today than they were 100, 1,000, or 2,000 years ago. So, while the market today is undervalued given current profits and interest rates, whether it goes up over time is a function of productivity growth.

The good news is that amidst the carnage in the economy today, there is one very bright spot—productivity growth. During the 10 years ending in March 1983, non-farm productivity (the output per hour of labor) increased just 0.9 percent per year. During the 10 years ending in March 2009, the output per hour of labor was up 2.5 percent. And even with economic activity crumbling in the past year, nonfarm productivity is still up 1.9 percent.

This is not a surprise to anyone who has paid any attention to the power of networks. Cell phones have been around for a long time, but they are worth more today than they were when they were first rolled out to consumers because of the very fact that more people have them. Any network node experiences the same benefits with increased usage. In other words, the initial productivity gains of new technologies are smaller but as they become more utilized, the productivity gains leap.

The computer on your desk becomes worth more every day because it is connected to a network. Every new person on the network adds to the people you can reach. Every new addition to the web, every new application makes the computer on your desk worth more. And those applications, the ones you have access to, are being invented at an accelerating rate.

Marc Andreessen, founder of Netscape, painted an incredibly optimistic picture in a recent *Fortune* magazine article this way:

> Technology and software tools have driven down the cost of starting a tech company by more than 100 times compared with a couple of decades ago, when modern venture capital structures were put in place. A company that needed $20 million to get a product out the door in the late 1980s now needs just $200,000."[1]

Wow! Now that is a very powerful positive force for any pessimist to reckon with.

The Internet is still the wild, wild West, and a vast blank slate, but it is developing very rapidly. Every new application makes it more valuable, and while there are some big players who benefit hugely from that growth, such as Microsoft, Cisco, and Google, there are millions of small businesses that are staking out claims and providing new goods and services to grateful customers.

MagnetStreet is an Illinois-based company that started out little more than a decade ago making refrigerator magnets for realtors and college and professional sports teams. As housing boomed, so did MagnetStreet. They weren't prescient, but they were constantly utilizing new technology to simplify ordering and production. This led to a new market—weddings. The newly-in-love can download their pictures on the web and design and then order custom-made "save the date" magnets.

Delivery times have been cut from weeks to overnight. And once your friends have saved the date, MagnetStreet can use state-of-the-art digital printing technology to supply you with invitations (also ordered seamlessly on the Internet) to the wedding and, as the family grows, baby announcements (with pictures). As the real estate market melted down, this new product line saved the company and actually propelled it to new heights. None of this would have been possible before the Internet, but MagnetStreet utilized it to boost productivity and open up new markets that many of its competitors could not.

The bottom line is that advances in technology are a driving force behind long-term economic growth. This does not mean that the economy cannot or will not have recessions and problems. In fact, during the past nine years, the stock market has seen two of its worst bear markets in history. What it does mean is that the underlying momentum of the economy is still positive.

Demand-siders can't see this because they believe the consumer drives the economy. They are worried about debt, saving, and financial markets. Supply-siders can see it, at least most of them, and they understand that the trends are still very positive in this dynamic system of free enterprise. In fact, as costs fall for new companies, growth rates and productivity should accelerate even more than they have in recent years.

But Government Is Growing . . .

Wait a minute, some are saying, this dynamic system of free enterprise is under assault by massive increases in government spending, new regulations, the potential for national health care, a crazy climate tax called "cap and trade," and maybe even higher income taxes. How can the economy possibly grow? Won't these impediments to growth drive business overseas and make the United States less competitive? There is no way that the stock market can go up, they say, no way that the economy can grow. Even Arthur Laffer, a leader of the supply-side movement in the late 1970s and early 1980s, has authored a new book titled *The End of Prosperity* (Threshold Editions, 2008).

Arthur is not normally a pessimist, but the book title says it all. And he's not the only one. Many conservatives are negative on the economy, too. This is partly a political position. If all these negative things, these moves toward bigger government and higher taxes, are happening, how can the economy show any signs of life? To think or say anything different is considered blasphemy, right?

Well, I wish I could be ideological about this, but I can't. In the 1960s and 1970s, the direction of government policy was horrific. We had, in order: Presidents Johnson, Nixon, Ford, and Carter—oh man!—The Four Horsemen of the Apocalypse. Taken as a whole, the decade of the 1970s was not very good for capitalism, investors, or the economy. The stock market went nowhere for the decade, and both inflation and unemployment rose above 10 percent. The word *stagflation* was invented, and people really thought the United States was done, finito, cooked. The sun was setting on the empire.

But, as we reviewed earlier in this chapter, the stock market and the economy roared in 1975–1976 when the Fed was easy. Then the market flattened out again until policies changed for the better. Once Reagan became president, the markets had one of their greatest runs ever. This rally stalled in the early 1990s, during the first few years of the first term of Bill Clinton. Many thought the end was nigh. But it wasn't. And the bull market of the 1990s got under way.

I am not saying that government policies don't matter. They do. In fact, before I leave you, I will review the things that government might do that could actually snatch defeat from the jaws of victory. But most of those policies have not yet been passed by Congress. And if they do pass, they will take years to have any major impact.

There is a big difference between a political fight over policy, such as the debates currently swirling around the Obama policies, and an investment strategy that can make money. Yes, the policies are bad. And yes, despite this, the market and economy can still go up in the near term.

That's were we are today. The stock market and economy are going to bounce strongly from panic lows seen at the end of 2008 and early 2009. A great deal of money is going to be made by those who can think strategically and optimistically, and not get caught climbing into a hole, buying gold, and hunkering down.

Chapter 10

Investing in the Midst of Mayhem

W*arning from the Economic Surgeon General:* This book was written in the summer of 2009. Because of the lag between writing and publication, by the time you read it, market prices will have changed. Between March and September 2009, the broad stock market indices rallied by more than 50 percent and economic data had begun to turn upward. This book argues that a V-shaped recovery is in the cards and the market could easily increase another 40 percent within the next year. Nonetheless, many expect the market to falter and form a "W"-shaped market bottom. No matter which outcome has unfolded, it doesn't mean that opportunity has passed you by. Read on to see why.

The economy, just like any living or breathing thing, operates on two cycles—a secular or long-term cycle and a cyclical or short-term cycle. Long-term trends in the economy are driven by productivity growth and technology, while cyclical movements depend almost exclusively on monetary policy.

Sometimes it's easier to think of this in terms of a metaphor. So let's imagine that the economy is a marathon runner. Any runner, but especially those who race over long distances, must build a tremendous base to be successful. This means multiple thousands of miles of training, backed up by good eating and sleeping habits. Without solid training and discipline, you can't build a base and you can't compete, at least not with any true success.

In a metaphorical sense, the economic "base" is productivity, entrepreneurship, and technology. It's the ongoing ability of an economy to produce new wealth. And anything that interferes with entrepreneurial activity or reduces the incentives to innovate and create, diminishes performance. High tax rates, more regulation, and increased government spending are the equivalent of eating poorly and not resting. They sap energy and harm the underlying ability of the economy to operate. Like ankle weights or wind resistance, they slow the athlete down.

But even if this happens, there are ways to boost performance (at least temporarily). Athletes use steroids. The government uses monetary stimulus. When the economy slows, the Fed leans into the wind, creates new money, and cuts interest rates in order to boost economic activity. But this stimulus always comes with a price. Every short-term fix, whether it is drugs or the monetary equivalent (easy money), may boost performance in the short term but comes with a long-term price.

At first, monetary policy pumps up the economy. It's a magic elixir. That is, until the effects wear off. It's a sugar high that takes you up but drops you like a rock. Printing money cannot possibly create long-term wealth, but it can make people feel wealthier for a short time. Think about it. If printing money really did create wealth, then counterfeiting should, and probably would, be legal. But counterfeiting isn't legal because those who print money get something for nothing. Eventually, printing money results in higher inflation.

The Super-Easy Fed

This process is unfolding right now. In response to the recent crisis, the Fed cut the federal funds rate from 5.25 percent to basically zero. At the same time, it expanded its balance sheet by more than 100 percent, from $800 billion to over $2.2 trillion, as it bought assets (commercial paper, mortgage-backed securities, and even Treasuries) in an attempt to stimulate financial markets.

The Fed's balance sheet is just like any other bank, but with one huge exception: The Fed can create money out of thin air—it can produce its own liabilities. It then exchanges that money for assets, which injects new money into the economy. The Fed can also borrow money and use this leverage to expand its balance sheet just like any private entity. In fact, this is exactly what the Fed did during the recent financial crisis. It borrowed money directly from the Treasury, while it has also enticed banks to hold what are called *excess reserves* at the Fed by paying interest on those reserves.

Funding the Fed's operations by borrowing does not increase the money supply. All it does is shift assets from one set of hands to another. The Treasury borrows money from bond buyers and then transfers that money to the Fed, which in turn buys assets, putting the money right back into the economy. Banks place depositor money at the Fed, in the form of excess reserves, instead of lending it out, but the Fed turns right around and buys Treasury bonds, commercial paper, or mortgage-backed securities, which in effect is lending it out.

Some analysts argue that because the Fed has more than doubled the size of its balance sheet, hyperinflation will result. But because borrowing does not increase the money supply, this analysis overstates the case. While it is certainly true that inflation is heading higher, hyperinflation or a collapse in the U.S. dollar is not in the cards, at least not anytime soon. Current monetary policy is accommodative, inflationary, and soft, but it is not hyperaccommodative or hyperinflationary. I expect overall consumer price inflation to end 2009 at roughly 2 percent, then accelerate to 3.5–4.0 percent in 2010 and 5.0–5.5 percent in 2011. Accelerating? Yes. But hyper? No.

But some argue with this forecast because they believe the opposite. Some analysts argue that paying interest on excess reserves takes money out of the financial system because banks are not lending those funds. This would be true if the Fed somehow held onto those reserves and did not put them right back into the economy. But the Fed takes in excess reserves and then uses them to expand its balance sheet. This money is cycled through the Fed, but it is not withdrawn from the banking system.

This use of the Fed balance sheet as a place to park assets is designed with the same purpose in mind as most of the crisis-induced Treasury programs—as an attempt to unfreeze the financial system. With mark-to-market accounting now reformed, the Fed's balance sheet is shrinking. But all of this is a sideshow to the really powerful part of what the Fed is doing—the actual creation of new money.

When the Fed creates new money out of thin air, it can buy assets and inject that money directly into the economy. Looking at the Fed's balance sheet suggests that about 85 percent of the expansion was accomplished by borrowing money, while about 15 percent of the expansion was accomplished by the creation of "new" money. This 15 percent represents a significant increase in the money supply and it has created a sea of liquidity, which is boosting economic activity very rapidly. Just like it did in 1975–1976, this easy money is also boosting the stock market.

Buy U.S. Stocks for the Short to Medium Term

On September 19, 2008, the day the $700 billion TARP plan was proposed by Hank Paulson, the Dow Jones Industrial Average was trading at 11,388, the S&P 500 was at 1,255, and the Nasdaq Composite was 2,274. As the panic unfolded, the market started to plummet. There was a brief bounce in December 2008, but no matter how much bailing out Washington, D.C., did, the markets continued to fall for six months.

Finally on March 9, 2009, the market hit bottom, with the Dow down 43 percent from September 19, to 6,547, the S&P 500 down

46 percent to 676, while the Nasdaq Composite was down 44 percent to just below 1,269. It wasn't a coincidence that these broad market indices all bottomed when it became clear that a bipartisan push from Congress would force the Financial Accounting Standards Board (FASB) to reform mark-to-market accounting. Panic began to recede, credit spreads narrowed, and in roughly three months, every stock index had retraced a V-shaped bounce of roughly 40 percent. Despite this bounce, the market was still undervalued by at least 40 percent, according to the capitalized profits model presented in Chapter 9.

People began referring to the "green shoots" of a recovering economy. This idea was first heard in early 2009 as economic data began to get better. But it was the wrong metaphor for what had really happened. The 2008 recession was not a normal recession—the grass and garden had not gone dormant. It was more like the grass and plants were stunned by a strong weed killer that held back growth (caused a panic) for a short period of time. The grass never died, it never went dormant; it was just stunned. A good watering was all it needed and that was provided by the Fed.

The recovery was always likely to be more robust and more rapid than the conventional wisdom expected. But because so many people misread the economy, thinking that capitalism had failed or that Great Depression II was right around the next corner, investors remained jittery. Any piece of data that was worse than expected spread fear, and every time the market moved down for a day or two the bears became convinced that the economy would not recover. The rise in stock prices was called a "dead cat bounce" or a "bear market rally," over and over again.

In a July 9, 2009, column, Nouriel Roubini wrote, ". . . the outlook for the U.S. and global economy remains extremely weak ahead. The recent rally in global equities, commodities and credit may soon fizzle out. . . ."[1] For reference, Roubini had predicted a recession would follow Hurricane Katrina, too. He has been bearish for a very long time.

But as long as mark-to-market accounting is held at bay, the threat of another shoe falling (another panic) is very, very small. And with the capitalized profits model and the Fed interest rate model both signaling the path upward, the market has a very nice wind at its back. An undervalued market does not mean that equity prices are guaranteed to go higher, but it does suggest that the odds of a stock rally are greater than the odds of another drop in prices.

And remember, the market can move up quickly, so waiting for a double-dip or trying to time the market is a recipe for underperformance. The Panic of 2008 led to an extreme drop in the market and a velocity-induced slump in economic activity. If the bears were right and this signaled an end to the world as we knew it, then a wimpy bottom was likely or perhaps even further declines in stock prices.

But the views presented in this book would suggest the opposite. When the economy turned, when the markets realized that capitalism was still alive and well and that the pessimists had exaggerated again, a melt-up in the market was a very real possibility. And this is exactly what happened between March and September 2009. But even with the Dow over 9,000 in mid-September it was still undervalued by 40 percent.

Before this rally is over, the stock market is likely to return to its pre-panic levels of early September 2008—possibly higher. If markets have reached their fundamental value by the time this book makes it into your hands, this does not mean that there are no more opportunities for stocks. With a strong economy behind them, earnings are set to rise in the second half of 2009 and into 2010. This will push up the market's fundamental value even further. While it will take a number of things going right, the Dow could easily move back to its old highs above 14,000 in the next few years.

Easy money alone will not be enough to push the market that high because the benefits from easy money are likely to last only through the end of 2010. If the Fed remains accommodative for longer than that, inflation rates will begin moving significantly higher, which will rob the economy of some of its strength. In the 1970s, it is clear that the rally stalled after 1976 and the stock market struggled from then until 1982.

And like the 1970s, politicians are very active. The Obama administration is moving rapidly to pass a national health care proposal and a carbon tax (cap and trade), both of which would limit the extent to which any stock market rally could actually continue after the impact of easy money dissipates. However, we do not know what policies will actually become law. Political winds can change suddenly.

President Clinton's attempt at pushing through a liberal agenda failed in 1994. The congressional elections of that year went against him and he changed. In 1995, Clinton said, "The era of big government is over." Between 1994 and 1998—the middle four years—the Clinton administration was the most economically conservative administration we have seen since Ronald Reagan—certainly more conservative than either Bush administration.

It is true that there is a much stronger populist drift in the nation these days than in the early 1990s. However, the United States is not yet willing to embrace socialism. This is why the more President Obama tries to push a very liberal agenda, the higher his unfavorable ratings climb and the lower his favorable ratings fall. As a result, the passage of all these dramatic big-government programs remains in doubt. And if these programs die a political death, then the market will get a very nice updraft in the years ahead.

Even if they do pass, the true cost to the economy, the real impact, will not be seen for years. Even the rollback of the Bush tax cuts, which is almost a certainty, will not occur until 2011. The bottom line is that for the next 12 to 18 months, the upward drift in equity prices will remain hard to stop. In the short term, easy money trumps bad fiscal policy, especially when the impact of that bad fiscal policy is years down the road.

Stocks for the Long Term: Small Cap, Value, and Momentum

Right now being long stocks will be profitable. Cash will underperform. But once stock market indices rise back to their fundamental value, and if government does not stop growing, a stock-picking strategy will become more important. In the late 1970s, when the nation was paying a huge price for drifting away from capitalism, small-cap stocks outperformed large-cap stocks, and value stocks outperformed growth stocks. In addition, Value Line[2] stock picks, which depend greatly on momentum, performed extremely well in the 1970s, especially late in the decade. Peter Lynch at Fidelity and Warren Buffett at Berkshire Hathaway also did very well in the 1970s.

When the world moves into the fiscal policy wilderness, like it did in the 1970s, investing in broad market averages (what people call indexing) is not the right thing to do. In other words, the government makes things tough for the average investor. In times like these, stock selection is even more important. Beating the averages is possible in this environment, but to do so takes a great deal of work.

It takes mental discipline and a careful and deliberative approach. But having good tools (databases, research, and computer power) is necessary, too. Most people are constitutionally incapable of doing this because of human emotion. The average person buys high and sells low. As a result, most investors would be better off having faith in a solid financial adviser who can make nonemotional, quantitative decisions. Sitting in cash, or just buying an index, is giving up. If you sit in cash, you will never make up any losses, you will never have the kinds of returns that are needed for retirement, you will never get ahead. And if you just buy an index, you will be blown around by the winds of government policy. So invest in good companies that can make profits despite the environment.

Small companies typically operate in niche markets, not broad, commodity-like markets. As a result, they tend to have more pricing power than larger companies. Small companies are more nimble and are able to dance through the regulatory minefield more easily. Small companies tend to be new in markets and therefore are also likely to be on the cutting edge of technology, which means they tend to grow faster than the economy as a whole. By definition, technology and productivity help grow profits over time.

In addition, many academic studies have shown that value stocks have consistently outperformed growth stocks and the market as a whole, but no one can say exactly how this happens. Why do investors overlook these companies in the first place, and how do they eventually find them so that their prices can be bid up? We don't know, but we do know that a rigorous, disciplined, and quantitative approach to searching them out is the best way to capture this upside over long periods of time. In the 1930s, and again in the 1970s, the market rewarded investors who picked their spots carefully.

Inflation Plays for the Medium and Longer Term

One thing that is almost a foregone conclusion is that inflation is heading higher. This flies in the face of conventional wisdom, which expected deflation to appear during the Panic of 2008. But this was the dog that didn't bark. Despite a sharp drop in commodity prices, especially oil and gas, which dragged down overall measures of inflation, noncommodity prices never did fall. As can be seen in Figure 10.1, producer and consumer prices, excluding food and energy (what we economists call "core" inflation), stayed relatively stable, and well above deflationary levels, even though the economy collapsed.

Many analysts still believe that it was the drop in economic growth during the Great Depression that caused deflation, but this was never true. Deflation in the 1930s was caused by a collapse in the money

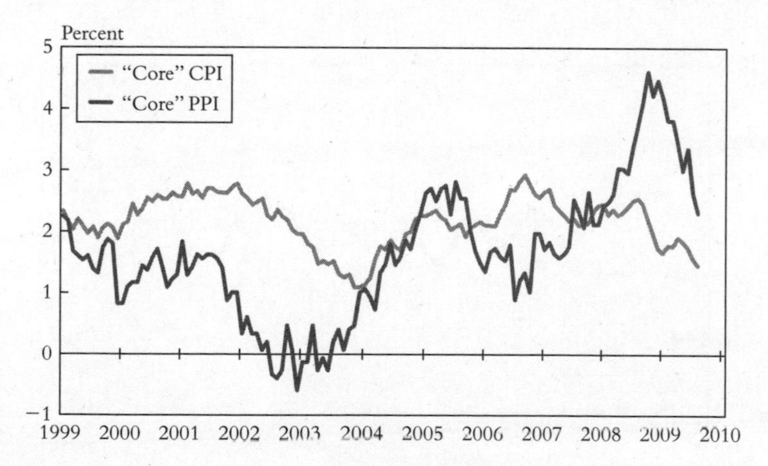

Figure 10.1 "Core" Consumer and Producer Prices
SOURCE: Bureau of Labor Statistics

supply. Today, the Fed has not made that mistake. In fact, it has made the opposite mistake. Monetary policy is so accommodative, it's as if the athlete were getting no sleep at all and injecting steroids like crazy. As a result, inflation is on its way.

It is true that commodity prices plummeted in the late 2008 and early 2009, but this was a temporary decline caused by a drop in the velocity of money. Now that the economy has stabilized, velocity is returning, and the Fed is easy, these inflationary trends in commodity prices will reassert themselves. Look at the long-term trends. Figure 10.2 shows that commodity prices rose sharply during the 1970s when the Fed was holding the federal funds rate below the natural rate. Commodity prices stabilized during the 1980s and 1990s when the Fed was holding the federal funds rate above or equal to the natural rate. And commodity prices have climbed again since 2001 as the Fed has once again followed an accommodative monetary policy.

The Fed talks of an "exit strategy"—and seems to believe that it can shrink its balance sheet before inflation starts to rise. But this is much easier said than done. The Fed really needs two exit strategies. One is relatively easy. The Fed can allow its asset purchases to wind down, and it can pay back the money that it borrowed at the same time. In fact, this was happening already in early 2009. Once mark-to-market

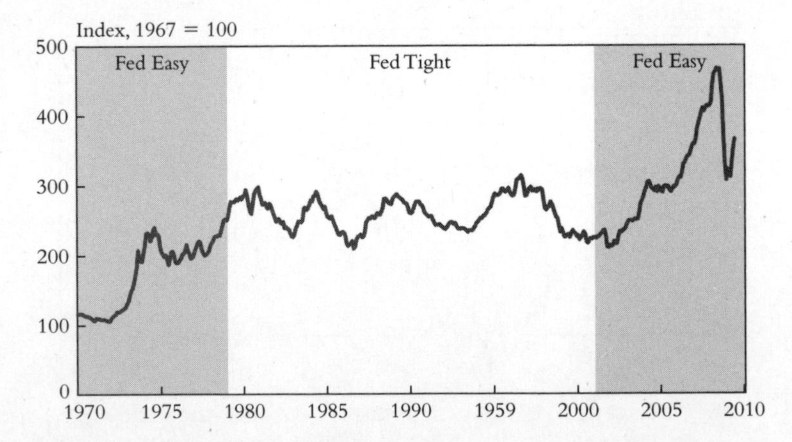

Figure 10.2 CRB Spot Commodity Price Index: All Commodities
SOURCE: Reuters-CRB Commodity Index Report

accounting was relaxed, the need for the Fed to involve itself in the market was diminished. By spring 2009, the Fed was already paying down Treasury debt and allowing some excess reserves to run off.

But the second step is much harder. Once the Fed has paid back all the Treasury loans and allowed all excess reserves to drain off, it will still hold assets that it purchased with printed (created) money. If it reverses these transactions it will be tightening monetary policy outright. It will be shrinking the money supply.

This is the equivalent of the FBI's coming for Sam and his $100 bills. If the Fed actually does drain money from the economy, the process will be painful. Getting hooked on drugs is easy, but getting unhooked is not. There is no painless way to reverse course once that new money is cycling inside the economy.

But the Fed will try to do this at some point. And when they do, they will have to have more fortitude than most central bankers have ever been able to stomach. In the 1970s, every time the Fed tried to back off its easy money, the political cacophony became so intense that it reversed course and cut rates again. This, of course, just led to higher inflation. Not until Paul Volcker was there a central banker who was tough enough to do what was necessary.

Whether Ben Bernanke, who has now been reappointed by President Obama to a new term as Fed Chairman, has this kind of fortitude is an open question. History suggests that it is unlikely. Because the Fed operates under a dual mandate—one that says it must pay attention to both inflation and unemployment—the political pressure is great. Imagine the Fed's trying to lift interest rates if the unemployment rate is still above 7 percent. The only central banks around the world that are seemingly able to run a monetary policy focused on inflation are the ones with a single mandate—a single focus on inflation—such as the European Central Bank.

Because the exit strategy will be more difficult than many believe, it is fairly easy to forecast that inflation will head higher in both the medium term and the long term. This suggests an investment strategy that steers clear of long-term bonds and focuses on investments that protect against inflation. Investing in one particular commodity, like gold, or one sector, like energy, may seem easy, but it is much better to invest in a broad basket of commodities. In addition, real estate will be an effective hedge against inflation. Yes, I said real estate. In an inflationary environment, your home and other real estate, like farmland, should help to hedge your assets against inflation. Prices are bottoming and in some areas are likely to rise significantly in the years ahead.

While some worry about a potential decline (even collapse) in the value of the dollar, these fears are probably overdone. Currency values are determined by the supply and demand for that currency, and it is clear that the supply of dollars has increased dramatically. However, the supply of euros, yen, British pounds, and just about every other currency in the world has also increased dramatically.

This means that these major currencies will all fall in value relative to goods and services. In other words, inflation will occur in just about every country, but if inflation is equal across countries, exchange rates will not change in any dramatic fashion. Big movements in exchange rates require significant differences in underlying inflation rates. As long as everyone is printing money and inflating, there is no reason to expect any sharp movements, let alone a collapse in the value of the dollar.

Foreign Equities

Those who do expect a sharp decline in the value of the dollar suggest that investors heavily weight foreign equities in any portfolio as a hedge against currency risk. But do not do this just because of a currency forecast. The dollar is unlikely to collapse because America is unlikely to collapse.

Nonetheless, there are still plenty of good fundamental reasons to invest overseas. First, many overseas equity markets became equally undervalued in recent years. Second, while most countries pushed stimulus and bailout packages, they were typically much smaller than those in the United States. This is good news—for them. Most countries will not have the significant pressure to hike tax rates that the United States will have in the years ahead. Third, globalization will continue despite fears of protectionism; and fourth, technology will continue to benefit all economies, but especially emerging markets, in a significant way.

Exchange-traded funds make it easy to invest overseas, and today's technology makes buying stocks directly on foreign exchanges uncomplicated. One thing to always remember is that once you choose the portion of your portfolio that will be invested in any market or sector, say emerging markets, you must remember to rebalance every 3, 6, or 12 months. Emerging markets, especially, can be volatile, and rebalancing forces you to take profits when times are good and buy cheap when times are tough.

Another thing to remember about foreign equity exposure is that most large and many small companies in the United States do a significant amount of global business. In the first half of 2009, about 45 percent of revenues for the S&P 500 came from overseas. In other words, investing in domestic U.S. equities provides significant international exposure. Foreign companies also do a significant amount of business in the United States, so investing globally does not remove U.S. exposure.

It used to be that foreign investing was justified because it provided diversification, and foreign markets often moved in contrary fashion to American markets. But convergence seems to be the name of the game these days, with markets around the globe moving in tandem rather than in opposition. This could change, but for right now it seems that world stock markets rise and fall as one.

As a result, investing overseas does not always provide diversification when you need it most. So one thing to look for when investing in foreign economies is a movement toward freedom. China and India, and many other developing nations, have been freeing up their economies for years. As a result, they are benefiting from strong global investment flows and from an entrepreneurial spirit that is blossoming heartily.

At the same time, Canada, Australia, New Zealand, the United Kingdom, and Ireland, along with much of continental Europe, have realized the mistakes of a social welfare state and are moving away from big-government policies. With the United States seemingly moving in the opposite direction, a great way to protect against this is to invest overseas. After all, if I can buy a foreign company that pays lower corporate tax rates but does business in America, instead of its U.S.-based competitor, why not do so?

Fixed Income

There are many developments that impact interest rates, but the most important is inflation. If inflation is high, interest rates will most likely be high. If inflation is low, interest rates will be low. And all of this is determined by Fed policy. In the 1960s and 1970s, when the Fed was holding short-term interest rates artificially low, inflation was rising, which pushed up long-term interest rates. As can be seen in Figure 10.3, the 10-year Treasury bond yield rose consistently between 1960 and the early 1980s.

Then monetary policy, under Volcker and then Greenspan, turned restrictive. This brought down inflation and interest rates. Like commodity prices, interest rates remained in a downtrend for decades. This was a golden era for U.S. bond investors. But the Fed came full circle, and it began to follow an easy monetary policy again in the early 2000s.

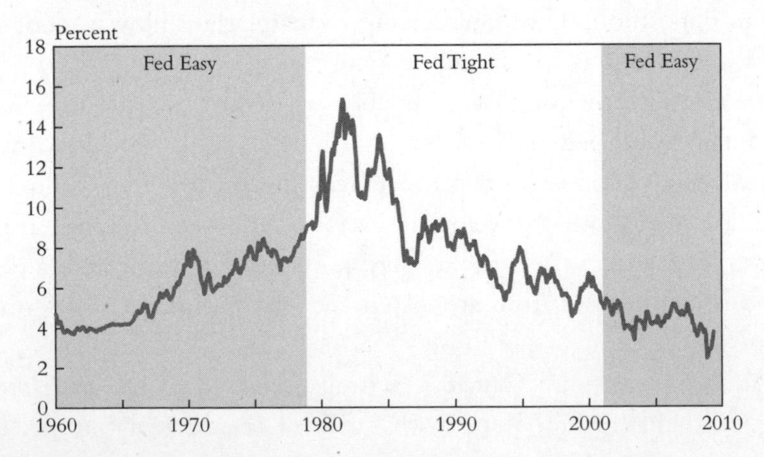

Figure 10.3 10-Year Treasury Note Yield
SOURCE: Federal Reserve Board

Commodity prices and inflation started to rise, and the long boom in bond markets appeared to come to an end in 2003. The 10-year Treasury yield hit a low of 3.1 percent in mid-2003, but had climbed to 5.1 percent by mid-2006. This increase in yields was driven partially by Fed rate hikes (starting in 2004), but also by fear of inflation. It stopped when the housing crisis started to unfold and gathered steam during the Panic of 2008. There is nothing like a good panic and a "flight to safety" for driving Treasury yields down and the 10-year Treasury yield bottomed at roughly 2.5 percent in December 2008. See Figure 10.4.

Now that the panic is over and the economy is growing again, the "flight to safety" is ending. The Fed is thinking about exit strategies that will at some point mean raising short-term interest rates. And because of the super-easy monetary policy, inflationary pressures will likely begin to appear. As a result, we are in the early innings of a long-term increase in U.S. Treasury bond yields.

The second factor that impacts interest rates is the risk of default. Treasury bonds have zero risk of default, no matter how many scary stories you hear about the United States losing its triple-A rating. However, corporate bond risks have understandably risen dramatically in recent years. Figure 10.5 shows 10-year maturity, BBB-rated corporate bond yields versus Treasury yields. As can be seen, the spread

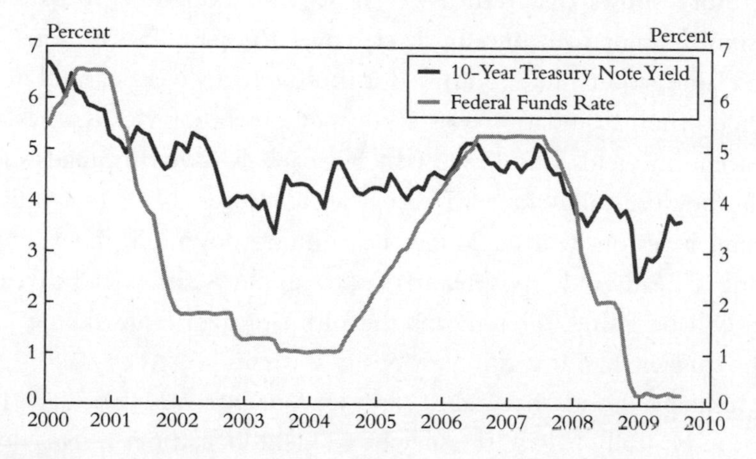

Figure 10.4 10-Year Treasury Note Yield versus Fed Funds Rate
SOURCE: Federal Reserve Board

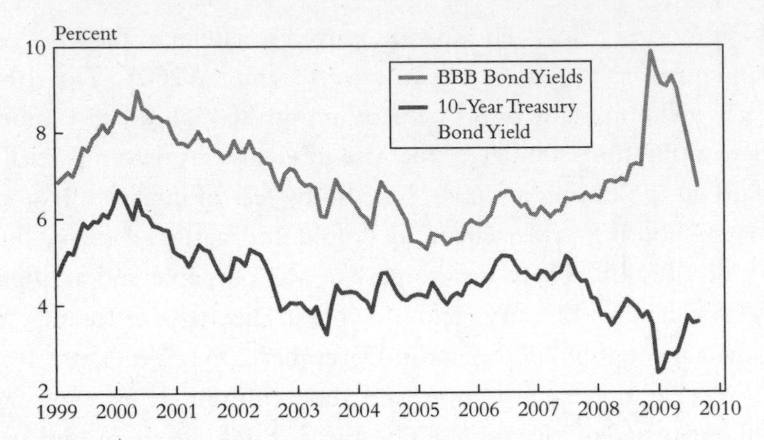

Figure 10.5 BBB Industrial Bond Yield versus 10-Year Treasury Note Yield
SOURCE: S&P/GIFR, Federal Reserve Board

between these corporate rates and the Treasury yield widened considerably in 2007 and 2008, but has narrowed sharply in 2009.

But even though the spread has narrowed, the market is still paying significantly more to anyone willing to hold corporate debt. These wide spreads have always presented a huge opportunity to those investors willing to step in at the height of a crisis and buy. Both the spread and the actual yield have come down, and they will eventually return to a level more typical of past recoveries.

History shows that returns to those who bought corporate debt at a similar point in economic cycles over the past 25–30 years have earned large, equity-like returns. But those returns were earned during a period when disinflation was a constant. In other words, the long-term trend in yields was down, which meant that when spreads started to fall, they typically chased Treasury yields lower. Now that inflation is rising, investors will no longer be running downhill. They will be fighting a headwind. As spreads narrow in the years ahead, Treasury yields will be rising. This means the ultimate gain from falling yields will be smaller than it was in past business cycles.

Municipal bonds have also experienced extreme volatility. Their yields are typically below Treasury bond yields because investors do not pay federal income taxes on municipal bond interest. This means that investors are willing to accept lower yields from a municipality than from the U.S. Treasury—not because these entities are less risky than the federal government, but because of the tax savings.

But, in 2008, in a very rare development, municipal bond yields rose significantly above Treasury yields. As can be seen in Figure 10.6, this lasted for about one year. Investors were very nervous that falling revenue from real estate taxes, sales taxes, and income taxes at the state and local level would leave some entities unable to take care of their debt. These fears dissipated in mid-2009, when Treasury yields moved back above municipal yields and the relationship returned to near normal.

The fact that spreads have come in from their widest levels does not mean that we are out of the woods as far as financial difficulties for municipalities or corporations. There are no guarantees. Defaults can and will happen, and they almost always lag the recovery. But the bond market has overpriced this risk, just like the stock market did. At the worst point in the Panic of 2008, the market was pricing in multiple Armageddons. And even though those spreads have now come in, they are still relatively wide.

As a result, there are opportunities for fixed-income investors willing to have faith in the economy. With inflation rising, however,

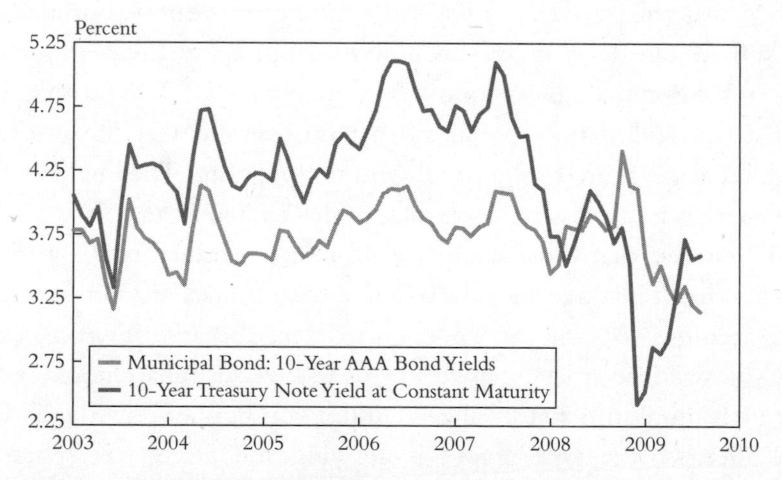

Figure 10.6 Municipal Bond Yield versus Treasury Yield 10-Year Maturities
SOURCE: Moody AAA-Rated Municipals, FRB, Delphis Hanover

it is important to think short term. As inflation and interest rates rise, having a shorter-term investment horizon allows you to reinvest, to roll over bonds, into higher yields. A disciplined approach of investing in bonds with maturities of between two and five years and then rolling the proceeds into new bonds as they mature is the best way to protect a portfolio from rising inflation.

Long-term bonds with a 20- or 30-year maturity will underperform as inflation increases. Inflation is the number one enemy of fixed-income investors, and it is coming back. After nearly three decades with the wind at their back, bond investors will be fighting an uphill, wind-in-your-face battle in the years ahead. There is no painless "exit strategy" for the Fed, and political pressure will likely push inflation up faster and further than many people think is possible.

Emotion and Investing

I can't tell you how to make a million dollars in the market (and I don't know anyone who can). I don't have a sure-fire investment strategy that guarantees huge returns—no one does. Twenty-seven years as an economist and analyst have shown me that there is no perfect investment strategy that will provide you positive returns every year of your life.

What I can do is show you how to think about the markets and their relationship to the economy. Along the way, I hope that I've helped you realize that capitalism isn't broken and that the future is bright. The bears are trying to tell you the opposite. They believe that the system is fatally flawed, especially in the United States.

If you fear that this is true, you can earn a return of 0.1 percent or 0.2 percent in three-month Treasury bills, money market funds, or bank accounts. And if you choose to do this because it's considered safe, you will lose at least 1 percent this year versus inflation and probably even more in the years ahead. And if you hunker down and "buy gold" because the government is growing and prices have risen so sharply in recent years, be careful. Gold has already quadrupled from its lows, and it's currently pricing in a great deal of future inflation.

There is no riskless way to increase wealth. But what we do know is that capitalism has led to consistent growth for more than two centuries. That growth has thrown off profits, and those profits have driven up the value of companies on the U.S. stock market. Because the equity market carries more risk than the bond market, its returns have been greater over time.

Many point to the fact that the stock market is still in roughly the same place today as it was 10 years ago as a sign that the future will not be bright. But that comparison takes the market from a point of extreme overvaluation and compares it to a period of extreme undervaluation. If you think the capitalist system is broken, if you really believe that, then you should not be investing at all. You should stay away from the markets altogether because if you don't trust capitalism, you don't trust people.

Entrepreneurs, the soul of capitalism, gamble very rarely. In fact, entrepreneurs make decisions that are designed to increase the odds of success and reduce the cost of failure. That's what they do. That's what builds a successful business. As a result, after trillions of decisions over hundreds of years, the economy that has been built is not fragile, brittle, weak, or shallow. It is strong, resilient, deep, and robust. It is built for stress.

Government caused the problems of 2008. Mark-to-market accounting caused banking failures that did not need to happen. The government response—dramatically cutting interest rates and spending trillions of dollars—morphed a significant problem in housing into a full-blown panic and catastrophe.

But a recovery is coming, and it will be stronger than conventional wisdom thinks possible. As a result, much of what has happened to asset prices in the past few years will be reversed. Fear drove down stock prices, pushed up credit spreads, dried up demand for real estate, and sent people scurrying for cover.

Yes, unemployment will peak near 10 percent, but that will not stop the economy from recovering. Stock prices will go back up, the spread between corporate bond yields and Treasuries will fall, the housing market will recover, and real estate prices will bottom. The economy will grow again and hope will return.

It is possible that the United States could move rapidly down the road to socialism. But this is not as likely as many fear. The United States is not a socialist country. In mid-2009 there were enough moderate Democrats in the House and Senate to stop the carbon tax and slow down national health care significantly—at least for the time being. The markets are still worried about these pieces of legislation and tax hikes, but there are two things to remember. First, they may not happen. The bills may die because the president's popularity is plummeting. Second, the real damage that they will do to the economy is still a ways off. In order to pass these pieces of legislation, Congress has back-loaded the costs onto future presidents and Congresses. The true expense won't hit for years. As a result, the near- and medium-term future is even brighter than it seems.

Chapter 11

The New Normal

On April 14, 2009, in a speech at Georgetown University, President Obama made reference to the Bible:

> There is a parable at the end of the Sermon on the Mount that tells the story of two men. The first built his house on a pile of sand, and it was destroyed as soon as the storm hit. But the second is known as the wise man, for when " . . . the rain descended, and the floods came, and the winds blew, and beat upon that house . . . it fell not: for it was founded upon a rock."
>
> We cannot rebuild this economy on the same pile of sand. We must build our house upon a rock. We must lay a new foundation for growth and prosperity—a foundation that will move us from an era of borrow and spend to one where we save and invest; where we consume less at home and send more exports abroad.

The storm that President Obama was referring to was mentioned earlier in his remarks that day, when he said, "[t]his recession was not caused by a normal downturn in the business cycle. It was caused by a perfect storm of irresponsibility and poor decision making. . . . " He then went on to propose new rules and regulations for Wall Street, plus huge new government spending initiatives for education, nationalized health care, and a carbon-based energy conservation tax. He suggested that each of these was a "pillar" of our new house upon a rock.

The president was, and is, clearly willing to blame the problems we have experienced in the past few years on capitalism, which he refers to as the sand. And with this argument he makes the case that government is the rock.

This argument is helped along by conventional wisdom that the United States is either in the midst of the next Great Depression or it will experience years of subpar growth, with above-average unemployment and below-average wage growth. Many, on both sides of the political aisle, think capitalism is broken or, at the least, has just become so complex that we must use government power to hold it in check so that it doesn't wreck everything. And no matter which one of these arguments you grab onto, the bottom line for the pessimists is that you can no longer really trust anyone or anything.

It's hard to tell who lost faith faster—the intellectual elite or the rank and file. But trust in the system broke down pretty darn quickly. Part of the reason for that is that just about every player in this saga has a dog in the fight.

- Politicians want power, and they get it when people are scared.
- Short-sellers like to make money, and they make it when stock prices fall.
- The press likes to report outlier stories of financial trouble and they get this in spades from short-sellers, who are a huge source for journalists.
- The Panic of 2008 convinced the press that the short-sellers and the pessimists were geniuses even though many of them had been bearish for many years prior to the panic and market crash.

- Talk radio likes a good enemy. And what better than socialism? With U.S. policy imitating France, it's easy to drum up fear and negativity.
- With the mainstream press, talk radio, politicians, and the short-sellers getting exactly what they wanted—negative excitement surrounding every broadcast—the "end of the world" dance was hard to stop.
- Finally, even people who wanted to be optimistic but had been scared into holding cash and missed the first 40 percent of the rally, wanted the market to go back down so that they could get in at those low prices again. They then convinced themselves that this would happen.

It was the perfect storm of negativity. Just about every opinion maker had a reason to believe in the conventional wisdom and remain firmly ensconced in the echo chamber of economic collapse. Anyone who dared to differ from the consensus was chastised and dismissed as out of touch. Even after the stock market had melted up in 2009, the bearishness continued because no one could believe it. This great confluence of negativity just couldn't be stopped.

One interesting response was that television journalists refused to call a 40+ percent rise in stock prices a bull market. When equity prices were falling in 2007 or 2008, the first time the market closed 10.0001 percent below its previous high, they were putting brightly colored banner headlines on television announcing the official onset of a bear market. But this didn't happen on the way up.

Pessimism was rampant, and capitalism was the whipping boy. And this fit perfectly into the populist drift of politics. The fact that the Obama administration and a Democratically controlled Congress are willing to blame capitalism is not a surprise. Many of them have spent their careers arguing for more government control of the economy. What is a surprise is that typically conservative columnists, politicians, economists, journalists, and intellectuals have been smitten by this conventional wisdom as well.

George W. Bush told CNN, "I've abandoned free-market principles to save the free market."[1] What can an economist say to that? We never did have completely free markets; it was government interference in them that caused the crisis. But Treasury Secretary Hank Paulson had convinced President Bush, just as he had convinced many other people, including most of the key journalists on the East Coast, that the U.S. financial system was about to fail. Paulson argued that intervention like this was the last thing he wanted to do. He didn't want to take over companies and risk hundreds of billions of dollars, but he had no choice. The system—capitalism—had let us down.

The underlying belief here is that consumers and businesses went off half-cocked and without proper supervision. They then made a hash of the world. Government argued that the economy needed "creative" public solutions to complex problems because it was the worst crisis in 80 years. And most importantly, we had to put aside our beliefs about free markets and capitalism for the time being to keep the system from completely collapsing.

David Brooks, conservative columnist for the *New York Times*, wrote that classical economic thinking didn't work and people weren't rational. He went so far as to call people "stupid."[2] Peggy Noonan, conservative writer for the *Wall Street Journal*, wrote a column titled "Goodbye Bland Affluence,"[3] in which she highlighted a couple who had moved to a farm in Michigan in an attempt to get away from the consumer-driven bland affluence of recent decades. In that column she wrote, "Many think that no matter how much money is sloshing through the system from Washington, creating waves that lead to upticks, the recession is really a depression. We won't 'come out of it,' as the phrase goes, for five or seven years, because the downturn is systemic, global, and because the old esprit is gone."[4]

Noonan wrote this in April 2009, disparaging the month-long equity rally as an "uptick." What Noonan referred to as the "old esprit" is a reference to what people thought was normal. Many others call what is going on today a search for "the new normal"—as in "Now that the system has completely crumbled, what will it look like when it is rebuilt?"

The list of those who gave up on capitalism is breathtaking. Somehow, many pundits began to equate capitalism with fragility, fraud, and failure. They not only lost faith in their fellow man, but they then turned on him as well—calling him bland, untrustworthy, and stupid. No wonder government exploded in size in such a short time frame. Government spending rose from 20 percent of gross domestic product (GDP) in 2007 to 26 percent of GDP in 2009, and hardly anyone batted an eye.

All of this is complete foolishness. Consumers are not irrational, and the economy is not broken. The vast majority of people are completely trustworthy. And those who understand capitalism—where it comes from, what causes it to work—have not lost faith. Capitalism is robust and reliable. It does not "fail."

Nonetheless, capitalism has brought so much good over such a long period of time that people have begun to take it for granted. They have forgotten that capitalism is the end and the means. The fruits of capitalism are so overwhelmingly delicious that we forget that the best part of the system is that it provides personal dignity. It allows men and women to find their most productive place in the world, while it lifts living standards to new heights. Nonetheless, many "conservative" columnists have joined with many politicians to make an argument that this crisis is so severe that the government must intervene. Even if we don't like what government is doing, it must be done.

Another interesting twist in the emotion department is that conservative politicians and pundits have become massively bearish as well. This is a reaction to President Obama's agenda, which leans pretty dramatically in the liberal direction. More government spending, higher taxes, and regulation all hurt the economy. The pundits are right that the direction of policy is negative for the economy over the long run, but I am afraid most of them do not make the distinction between long and short term.

Their bearishness is going to look pretty foolish in the next 12 to 18 months as the economy booms. The Fed is so easy that it will overcome any policy problems in the near term. This is reminiscent of the early 1990s, when President Clinton raised taxes and proposed a new health care plan. Talk radio predicted the Clinton recession, which never came. Why? Because the Fed was super-easy in the early 1990s.

The immediate data we see every morning when we roll out of bed have not been pretty. The unemployment rate is near 10 percent; defaults and foreclosures continue to rise; that house (or houses) down the street isn't selling. It has been a nasty recession. But it's not the end of the world. Because the panic took economic activity to such low levels, the bounce alone from that will lift economic activity dramatically in the quarters ahead. But, more importantly, capitalism itself will reassert itself and lift growth in the quarters beyond the bounce. The economy is set to surprise the conventional wisdom in dramatic fashion.

Big Government Hurts

As the next year or two unfold, there will be some very interesting cross-currents affecting markets and politics. First, easy money will lift the economy, which will convince many that the federal government stimulus spending and President Obama deserve credit for saving the economy. It's not true, but they will get credit anyway.

The more credit the president gets for helping the economy recover, the more likely his agenda can advance on Capitol Hill. That agenda includes a government takeover of the health care system, a huge tax on carbon emissions, and sharp increases in tax rates.

Unfortunately, we have experience with these kinds of policies already and they do not help the economy no matter how many times politicians say they do. Figure 11.1 shows government spending as a share of GDP versus the unemployment rate. As can be seen, the unemployment rate moves higher whenever government spending rises as a share of GDP.

The reason? Government must either borrow or tax every dollar it spends from the private sector. Therefore, the bigger share of the economy the government spends, the smaller the share of the economy left for the private sector. In the 1960s and 1970s, government spending moved up and down as Fed policy pushed the economy up and down, but government consistently grew over that 20-year period. As the public sector grew, the private sector became less vibrant. Productivity growth slowed, inflation rose, and in each recession, unemployment hit a new peak, finally rising to 10.8 percent in 1982.

Then, under Ronald Reagan and Bill Clinton, government spending fell as a share of GDP and unemployment fell to new lows. Every trough was lower and every peak was lower. This remained true right up through 2000, when under President Bush government spending started to rise again as a share of GDP. Now, the unemployment rate has moved up to a 25-year high, well above the last peak and a sign that the underlying economy is already paying a price for bigger government.

Some argue that the government spending and unemployment data shown in Figure 11.1 are correlated because when unemployment rises, government spending must rise, too. However, if we remove all the cyclical patterns from this data and compare underlying trends, it is clear that the natural rate of unemployment as estimated by the Congressional Budget Office rose consistently in the 1970s and fell in the 1980s and 1990s.

In the next few years, with government spending on the rise to a peacetime record share of GDP, the underlying unemployment rate will rise as well. Even though the economy is set to grow more rapidly

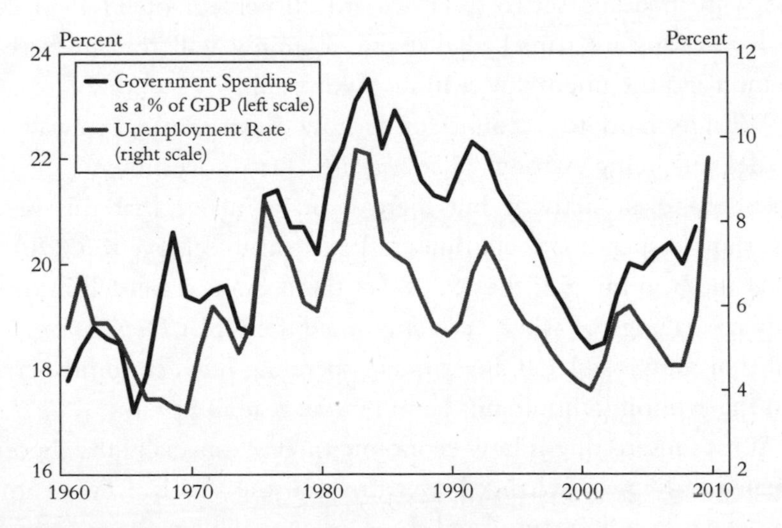

Figure 11.1 Government Spending versus Unemployment
Source: OMB, BLS

in the next 12 to 18 months, the unemployment rate will not come down to its recent lows, let alone any level remotely close to the trough of 3.9 percent seen in the late 1990s.

Keynes and Government

It's easy to understand why John Maynard Keynes is beloved by politicians and government bureaucrats. He argued very forcefully that the economy could not operate without government. To paraphrase, he thought that occasionally the consumer had a brain freeze. Animal spirits . . . you know. And when this happened, the government needed to spend. Without government, everything wobbled out of control. With it, the economy avoided big cyclical swings. What government bureaucrat wouldn't like that theory?

But now the Keynesians are worried. Government spending increased from 3.4 percent of GDP in 1930 to 10.5 percent in 1936 and the unemployment rate stayed very high anyway. In 2000, government spending was 18.8 percent of GDP. It had climbed to 20 percent in 2007 and then 21 percent in 2008. This spending was supposed to boost economic activity, but the economy fell into a recession anyway. And with spending set to spike toward 26 percent of GDP in 2009, the Keynesians are panicked that the economy will remain mired in the mud and the unemployment rate won't fall.

What is hard to account for is how Keynesians get away with decades of being wrong. They claim that government spending boosts economic activity, but there is no evidence that this is true. Government spending is six times as large today (relative to GDP) as it was at the beginning of the 1930s, yet the economy still fell into what many are calling the worst economy since the Great Depression. How could this be possible? If government spending lifts economic activity, then the economy should not be in recession at all.

What's interesting is how economic theory, especially the theory of deficit spending, has changed over time. In the 1930s, Keynes argued that deficit spending stimulated the economy. This was the essence of his theory of aggregate demand. When consumers would not spend, the government should deficit spend to make up the difference. Some even argue that there is a multiplier effect, so that every dollar of government spending created more than a dollar of economic activity.

Somewhere in the 1980s, however, this idea got lost when federal budget deficits appeared while Ronald Reagan was president. All of a sudden, deficits were thought to be harmful to the economy. According to many economists, the Reagan deficits "crowded out" private investment, pushed up interest rates, and hurt the economy. All of a sudden, deficits were bad, not good.

This view of deficits carried on through the 1990s. Robert Rubin and Bill Clinton were given credit for creating a budget surplus, lowering interest rates, and boosting economic activity. But now, apparently, economists have changed their minds again. Deficit spending in 2009, according to the Council of Economic Advisors, will boost growth and create jobs with no significant impact on inflation or interest rates. Whatever happened to "crowding out?"

Look, this is just a guess, but it seems that the economics profession and journalists who report on economics are persuaded by politics, not economics. How else is it possible to explain how deficits went from being good to bad to good again? This had nothing to do with a shift in the findings of academic research. It can be explained only by politics.

How Bad Can It Get?

National health care, cap and trade, tax hikes, income tax surcharges, the value-added tax, stimulus—the hits just keep on coming. But the fact that bad things are being proposed and may even become law does not mean that there are not huge opportunities in the future.

The Great Society, and what Lyndon Johnson called the War on Poverty, was begun in 1964. Welfare was ratcheted up significantly. Federal food stamps began, along with Head Start. In 1965, Medicare and Medicaid were begun. Government spending was put on a permanently faster path.

In the early 1970s, the United States took over Amtrak, closed the gold window, devalued the dollar, initiated wage and price controls, and enforced a top capital gains tax rate of 50 percent and top income tax rate of 70 percent. Inflation rose above 10 percent, and trucking, airlines, and banking were heavily regulated. The United States subsidized solar energy, enforced caps on energy prices at the wellhead, and increased the minimum wage multiple times. This was a horrible period for fiscal policy.

So how does it compare with today? Well, so far, the policies of the 1960s and 1970s are much worse than the policies of the early 2000s. Tax rates are significantly lower than they were in the 1970s, trade barriers are less burdensome, and regulation has been significantly reduced in just about every industry. While government spending has leapt to a post-WWII high, tax rates are scheduled to go up significantly, and there are many intrusive government proposals on the table, the impact of all this will not be felt for years.

Easy money is the Novocain of the economy. As long as the Fed is following an accommodative monetary policy, the market and economy will move up sharply. This is exactly what happened in 1975–1976 despite the fact that fiscal policies were headed in the wrong direction.

Roosevelt, Carter, or Clinton

Even with a strong tailwind and some early successes, the supporters of big government and President Obama's larger legislative agenda hit a wall in the summer of 2009. Cap and trade (a massive new carbon tax) was dead in the Senate after passing the House, and the health care bill was facing an uphill battle. One would think that the "failure of capitalism" and the "worst economic crisis in 80 years" would make passing any legislation pretty darn easy. But the American people are apparently not ready to throw in the towel. Democratic senators and representatives from conservative states and districts are very reluctant to pull the trigger on universal health care without more debate.

Part of the problem was that government had already increased spending by more in one year than it had since World War II. Federal spending rose from 21 percent of GDP in fiscal year 2008 to 26 percent in fiscal year 2009. The U.S. government will spend $4 trillion in fiscal year 2009—an increase of $1 trillion over 2008. The federal budget, if it were a country, would rank as the fourth largest GDP in the world—roughly the same size as China. In other words, 536 people in Washington, D.C. (435 House members, 100 senators, and one president) will spend as much money as 1 billion Chinese can produce. Just the $1 trillion increase in spending between 2008 and 2009 was the equivalent of annual GDP of Australia. In just one year, the United States spent an additional amount equal to the entire GDP of a well-developed country of 21 million people.

Everyone knows that the increase in spending must eventually be paid for by someone. So as the President began to push for universal health insurance, which will increase government spending by at least another trillion dollars, his approval ratings began to fall even though he has promised that 95 percent of Americans would not pay higher taxes.

But Americans know that all of this spending cannot be paid for by taxes on the top 5 percent of income earners. There is no possible way. According to the Tax Foundation, in 2007, the top 5 percent of income earners, only 7 million families, paid 60.6 percent of all income taxes. These families reported adjusted gross income of at least $160,000 per year, and in total they account for 37.4 percent of all income.[5] To attempt to close the deficit by raising only the tax rates of the top 5 percent of income earners would require a massive tax hike.

The government spends so much that the rich just don't have enough to support it. If the government confiscated the entire net worth of the Forbes 400—the 400 richest people in the United States—their $1.57 trillion[6] would not even support the federal budget for six months. The only way to close the deficit and pay for health care is to raise taxes on the middle class. More than one-half of all income is earned by families that report adjusted gross income between $32,000 and $160,000 per year.[7] Not taxing them is just not an option.

Once this is understood, the growth in government will hit a major roadblock. It remains a center-right country. As a result, the idea that government policy will move sharply leftward and the United States will start to resemble France is suspect. In fact, as the liberal agenda began to stumble in the Congress during the summer of 2009, the stock market seemed to gather more momentum. And if proposals for big government expansion can be defeated, the next few years will look much brighter indeed.

There were always three ways that the Obama administration could have gone. They could have followed the path of Franklin Roosevelt, or of Jimmy Carter, or of Bill Clinton. Roosevelt was able to rally support for massive government intervention in economic activity. Even though the unemployment rate remained high, he was able to continually shift blame onto Wall Street and the market system. This allowed him to push for even more government. The result was a disaster economically but a major political success for FDR.

Jimmy Carter was a fatalist. He assumed that the world as we knew it was ending and that it was his job to manage the decline. The world was running out of oil, unemployment and inflation would be permanently elevated, and we just had to accept that this was our lot in life. We just had bad timing. It was no big surprise that he served only one term. The optimistic Ronald Reagan took his place.

Bill Clinton was a truly successful Democrat who changed gears midstream. He raised taxes at first and attempted to impose health care reform. But then his numbers went down, and the midterm elections went against him and the Democrats. Bill Clinton turned into an economic conservative. Capital gains tax rates were cut, free trade was wholeheartedly endorsed, welfare was reformed, and government spending fell as a share of GDP. He won reelection in a landslide.

President Obama will end up governing like one of these past presidents. And it may be new technology, globalization, and the warp speed of our daily lives—what can be called "Internet Time"—that will determine which one. It is simple to dismiss Carter as the template—it just doesn't fit. Obama is not a fatalist. This leaves two potential paths—Roosevelt or Clinton.

Roosevelt got away with many government intrusions into the private sector in part because time moved more slowly. Today, everything is reported on in real time and everything happens faster. Blogs highlight every aspect of a new policy, the impact is seen globally, and the debate takes place in the bright lights of the public eye. Back in the 1930s, by the time someone could see the negative results of a piece of legislation, it was too late—it was years down the road. Today, all of this gets debated right up front and much of it can be seen—in Internet Time.

The first president who faced this pressure from Internet Time was Bill Clinton, and the impact was visible. It forced him to follow more right-leaning policies than he really wanted because that was the only way for him to serve a second term. The economy benefited greatly, and the stock market rallied. None of this was predictable when Bill Clinton was first elected, but in hindsight it is easy to see why it happened.

These are the pressures that Barack Obama will face. And Internet Time suggests that policies will not be as damaging to the economy as many fear. If Congress does not pass health care and environmental laws this year, it will be even more difficult next year because it is an election year. Politicians who want to pass universal health care are in a race against time. In other words, there is a very good chance that the truly damaging bills will never get passed.

By the time you read this, we will know (or have a very good idea) whether health care has passed or will pass this year. If it does, as we have noted before, the negative impact on the economy in the short or medium term will be small because the costs and burdens are backloaded.

The Future Still Looks Bright

In the end, there are many people who want you to believe that the Panic of 2008 was caused by market failure. They want you to believe that capitalism is unstable, that the entire U.S. economy is built upon shifting sand. They want you to believe that businesses can't be trusted but government can be. How any concept like this gains so much traction is a real mystery.

People do all of these things—they run businesses and they deliver government services. If a person cannot be trusted in business, what makes them any more trustworthy in government? If people are so unpredictable, greedy, stupid, and bland in the private sector, why would they be any different in government? It's a bit of a conundrum.

There is clear evidence that panics and depressions happened with some regularity back in the 1800s and early 1900s, and it is also true that government was small back then, but this does not mean that the economy was unstable. Government experimented with two different national banks, often changed the price of gold or silver, issued debt, and regularly interfered with the banking system. This does not prove that government caused those panics, but the idea that government was somehow nonexistent in the 1800s is simply not true.

The key is that the United States made it through all of that and has averaged a little more than 3 percent real GDP growth per year for the past 20, 50, 100, and 200 years. This history of free-market capitalism is a huge hurdle for anyone who wants to say that it was built on sand to overcome. The United States has created so much wealth and built such a robust system that taking it down is much more difficult that anyone thinks. In the end, the economy really is built on a rock. The new normal will look a lot like the old normal.

In other words: *It's Not as Bad as You Think.*

Notes

Introduction

1. Paul R. Krugman, *The Return of Depression Economics* (Boston: W. W. Norton & Company, 2000).
2. Harry S. Dent, *The Great Depression Ahead: How to Prosper in the Crash Following the Greatest Boom in History* (New York: Free Press, 2009).
3. Don Braby, *The Greatest Depression of All Time: Will America Survive This Time & What Can You Do About It* (CreateSpace, 2008).
4. Stathis, *America's Financial Apocalypse: How to Profit from the Next Great Depression* (Grand Rapids, MI: AVA, 2006).
5. Peter D. Schiff and John Downes, *Crash Proof: How to Profit from the Coming Economic Collapse* (Lynn Sonberg Books) (New York: John Wiley & Sons, 2007).
6. Michael Panzner, *Financial Armageddon: Protect Your Future from Economic Collapse* (Grand Rapids, MI: Kaplan, 2008).
7. Barack Obama, "Remarks by the President on the Economy." Speech at Georgetown University, Washington, D.C., April 14, 2009.

Chapter 1

1. Paul Krugman, "Reagan Did It," *New York Times*, May 31, 2009. www.nytimes.com/2009/06/01/opinion/01krugman.html.
2. *History of the Eighties—Lessons for the Future* (Washington, DC: Federal Deposit Insurance Corporation, 1997).

3. "Piling On."*The Economist*, May 30, 2009: 13.
4. Mark-to-market accounting (aka fair value accounting) is an accounting rule that forces the use of market prices in the calculation of a firm's income and net worth. The damaging part of this accounting rule is its application in an environment of capital regulations. When market prices for securities are used to calculate "regulatory capital," the impact on financial institutions can be dramatic.
5. Richard A. Posner, "Capitalism in Crisis,"*Wall Street Journal*, May 7, 2009, Opinion sec.: A17.
6. Armstrong Williams, "Between Scylla and Charybdis,"*Washington Times*, April 15, 2009. www.washingtontimes.com/news/2009/apr/15/between-scylla-and-charybdis/.
7. Amity Shlaes, *The Forgotten Man: A New History of the Great Depression* (New York: HarperCollins, 2007), 7–8.
8. Edmund Conway, "Geithner Insists Chinese Dollar Assets Are Safe," *UK Guardian,* June 1, 2009. www.telegraph.co.uk/finance/financetopics/financialcrisis/5423650/Geithner-insists-Chinese-dollar-assets-are-safe.html.

Chapter 2

1. John Maynard Keynes is perhaps the most famous economist to have ever lived. He became popular during the Great Depression, and the ideas laid out in his most famous book, *The General Theory of Employment, Interest and Money*, still dominate university teaching to this day. One reason he became and remains so famous is that he supported government interference in the economy to tame the business cycle. This, of course, found favor with politicians and bureaucrats the world over. What government official doesn't want to hear that growing the government can be good for the economy?
2. Milton Friedman, *There Is No Such Thing as a Free Lunch* (Chicago: Open Court Publishing Company, 1977).
3. Barack Obama, Press Conference by the President. White House East Room, Washington, DC, February 9, 2009. www.whitehouse.gov/the_press_office/PressConferencebythePresident/.
4. Thomas Malthus, *An Essay on the Principle of Population* (London: J. Johnson, in St. Paul's Church-yard, 1798).
5. Joseph A. Schumpeter, *Capitalism, Socialism, and Democracy* (New York: Harper Perennial, 1962).
6. Angus Maddison, *Contours of the World Economy 1–2030 AD: Essays in Macro-Economic History* (New York: Oxford University Press, 2007), 69.
7. Ibid.
8. Ibid., p. 81.

9. William Easterly, *The Elusive Quest for Growth* (Cambridge, MA: MIT Press, 2001), 175.
10. Arthur Sullivan and Steven M. Sheffrin, *Economics: Principles in Action* (Upper Saddle River, NJ: Pearson Prentice Hall, 2003), 6.
11. Ludwig von Mises, *The Anti-Capitalistic Mentality* (Princeton, NJ: Van Nostrand, 1956).
12. Maddison, *Contours of the World Economy*, pp. 313–314.
13. Douglass Cecil North, *Understanding the Process of Economic Change* (Princeton, NJ: Princeton University Press, 2005).

Chapter 3

1. Penelope Patsuris, "Detroit Puts B2B into Drive,"*Forbes*, November 12, 1999.
2. *Manufacturing News* 6(6), March 19, 1999. www.manufacturingnews.com/index.html.

Chapter 4

1. Edelman Trust Barometer, 2009 Edition, www.edelman.com/speak_up/blog/Trust_Barometer_Executive_Summary_FINAL.pdf.
2. Alan Greenspan, "Balance of Payments Imbalances." The Per Jacobsson Lecture. www.iadb.org/intal/intalcdi/PE/2009/02532.pdf.
3. "BNP Paribas Investment Partners Temporarily Suspends the Calculation of the Net Asset Value of the Following Funds: Parvest Dynamic ABS, BNP Paribas ABS EURIBOR and BNP Paribas ABS EONIA."*BNP Paribas*, August 9, 2007.
4. President George W. Bush, Georgetown University, October 15, 2002, President Hosts Conference on Minority Homeownership.
5. Edward Gramlich, "Booms and Busts: The Case of the Subprime Mortgage." Speech at Kansas City Federal Reserve Annual Jackson Hole Symposium, August 31, 2007.
6. Peter Wallison, *Critical Review* 21(2–3), 2009, 366–369. Routledge Taylor & Francis Group.
7. Lawrence B. Lindsey, "The KISS Rule for Markets,"*Wall Street Journal*, April 2, 2008.
8. Alan Greenspan, Federal Reserve System's Fourth Annual Community Affairs Research Conference, Washington, D.C. April 8, 2005, *Consumer Finance*. www.federalreserve.gov/boarddocs/speeches/2005/20050408/default.htm.
9. Steve Liesman, CNBC *Squawk Box*, June 17, 2009. www.cnbc.com/id/15840232?video=1155549236&play=1.

Chapter 5

1. David Brooks, "An Economy of Faith and Trust," *New York Times*, January 6, 2009.
2. David Brooks, "The Great Unwinding," *New York Times*, June 11, 2009, www.nytimes.com/2009/06/12/opinion/12brooks.html.
3. John M. Keynes, *The General Theory of Employment, Interest and Money* (London: Macmillan, 1936), 161–162.
4. Jean Baptiste Say was a French economist who lived from 1767 to 1832. In his "Treatise on Political Economy," he outlined Say's law, which says "the supply (sale) of X creates the demand (purchase) of Y."
5. Ludwig von Mises was the father of Austrian economics. It was his work that influenced the Nobel Prize–winning work of economist F.A. Hayek. Von Mises was born in 1881 and lived until 1973. He is responsible for the treatise "Human Action." This piece, along with many of his works, dealt with monetary economics and inflation as well as the differences between government-controlled economies and free trade.
6. Percy L. Greaves, *Mises Made Easier: A Glossary for Ludwig Von Mises' Human Action* (Dobbs Ferry, NY: Free Market Books, 1974), 69.
7. Ben Bernanke, Federal Reserve Board, "The Global Savings Glut and the U.S. Current Account Deficit." Speech on March 10, 2005.
8. *History of the Eighties—Lessons for the Future* (Washington, DC: Federal Deposit Insurance Corporation, 1997).
9. Richard F. Janssen, "Third World's Debts, Totaling $500 Billion, May Pose Big Dangers," *Wall Street Journal* [Princeton] January 28, 1981, p. 1.

Chapter 6

1. AMLF: Asset-Backed Commercial Paper Money Market Mutual Fund Liquidity Facility.

   CAP: Capital Assistance Program

   CPFF: Commercial Paper Funding Facility

   MMIFF: Money Market Investor Funding Facility

   PDCF: Primary Dealer Credit Facility

   PPIP: Public-Private Partnership Investment Program

   TAF: Term Auction Facility

   TALF: Term Asset-Backed Securities Loan Facility

   TARP: Troubled Assets Relief Program

   TLGP: Temporary Liquidity Guarantee Program

   TSLF: Term Securities Lending Facility
2. Tom Robbins, *Even Cowgirls Get the Blues* (New York: Bantam Books, 1976), p. 1.

3. Larry Summers, "Reflections on Economic Policy in Time of Crisis." Speech, Council on Foreign Relations. *Wall Street Journal*, June 12, 2009. http://blogs.wsj.com/economics/2009/06/12/summers-remarks-at-council-on-foreign-relations/.
4. C. William Thomas, "The Rise and Fall of Enron,"*Journal of Accountancy*, April 2002.
5. Ibid.
6. SEC, Staff. *Report and Recommendations Pursuant to Study on Mark to Market Accounting*. Rep. October 8, 2008. www.sec.gov/news/studies/2008/marktomarket123008.pdf.
7. Ibid.
8. Milton Friedman and Anna Jacobson Schwartz, *A Monetary History of the United States, 1867–1960* (Princeton, NJ: Princeton University Press, 1963), 355.
9. L. William Seidman, *Full Faith and Credit: The Great S&L Debacle and other Washington Sagas* (New York: Crown, 1993), 128.

Chapter 7

1. John Waggoner, *USA Today*, November 17, 2008. www.usatoday.com/money/perfi/basics/2008-09-16-damage_N.htm
2. Cindy Perman, CNBC.com, September 29, 2008, www.cnbc.com/id/26945972/.
3. Vikas Bajaj and Michael Grynbaum, "For Stocks, Worst Single-Day Drop in Two Decades,"*New York Times*, September 29, 2008.
4. George W. Bush, "Address to the Nation on Financial Markets." Washington, DC, September 24, 2008.
5. Ibid.
6. Ibid.
7. Ben S. Bernanke, "Financial Reform to Address Sytemic Risk." Speech, Council on Foreign Relations, Washington DC: Board of Governors of the Federal Reserve System. March 10, 2009. www.federalreserve.gov/newsevents/speech/bernanke20090310a.htm.

Chapter 8

1. Nouriel Roubini, "The United States of Ponzi."*Forbes*, March 18, 2009. www.forbes.com/2009/03/18/american-economy-housing-bubble-madoff-opinions-columnists-ponzi.html.
2. David Brooks, "The Great Unwinding,"*New York Times*, June 11, 2009. www.nytimes.com/2009/06/12/opinion/12brooks.html.
3. Ibid.

4. Robert Shiller, "Thrifty China, Spendthrift America,"*Project Syndicate*, August 2006. www.project-syndicate.org/commentary/shiller40.
5. Ludwig von Mises, *The Anti-Capitalistic Mentality* (Princeton, NJ: Van Nostrand, 1956), 3–4.

Chapter 9

1. Kevin Maney, "Marc Andreessen Puts His Money Where His Mouth Is,"*Fortune*, July 20, 2009, p. 42.

Chapter 10

1. Nouriel Roubini, "Brown Manure, Not Green Shoots," July 9, 2009, www.forbes.com/2009/07/08/jobs-report-mortgages-unemployment-recession-opinions-columnists-nouriel-roubini.html.
2. Value Line is an independent research company founded in 1931. Today, it employs approximately 80 professional security analysts and statisticians, who scour the stock market with proprietary models to find stocks that have a chance of outperforming the market. Its models performed extremely well in the 1970s.

Chapter 11

1. George W. Bush, interview on CNN, December 16, 2008, www.breitbart.com/article.php?id=081216215816.8g97981o&show_article=1.
2. David Brooks, "Greed and Stupidity,"*New York Times*, April 2, 2009.
3. Peggy Noonan, "Goodbye Bland Affluence,"*Wall Street Journal*, April 17, 2009.
4. Ibid.
5. Tax Foundation, Summary of Latest Federal Individual Income Tax Data, July 30, 2009. www.taxfoundation.org/publications/show/250.html.
6. Matthew Miller and Duncan Greenberg, "The Forbes 400 Richest Americans," *Forbes*, September 17, 2008. www.forbes.com/2008/09/16/forbes-400-billionaires-lists-400list08_cx_mn_0917richamericans_land.html.
7. Tax Foundation, Summary of Latest Federal Individual Income Tax Data.

Acknowledgments

My love affair with economics started in my very first university class on the subject. I never looked back. I never wanted to do anything else. For that, I thank the Lord. I was blessed with direction—a place to focus my energy. I was also blessed with great teachers, including Professor John Wicks at the University of Montana. His class in empirical research design, his "dinging," and his famous Seven Ps prepared me well to participate in the real world.

At the beginning of our careers, we come armed with certain tools and stand at the back of the crowd. No one even knows we are there. We start tapping people on the shoulder, asking them if we can help in whatever it is they are doing. If we do a good job, we get referred to someone else or asked to do something else. Slowly, the crowd parts and lets us in. It eventually closes ranks behind us, pushing us forward and cheering us on.

And over the years, I have had the pleasure of being cheered on by some great businessmen and women—at the Harris Bank, United States Senate, and Griffin, Kubik, Stephens and Thompson, Inc. However, this book would have never seen the light of day without Jim Bowen, founder and president of First Trust in Wheaton, Illinois.

Jim is a true entrepreneur, with an uncanny ability as a leader to get the most from people. He has a servant's heart and has designed First Trust to "travel through time with people." His influence and positive attitude can be found on just about every page of this book. Our friends, the clients of First Trust, can also take ownership in this book. It was their penetrating questions and need to dig deep for truth that pushed me every time I sat down to write. I hope I have fulfilled their expectations.

Of course, no book exists on writing alone. At home, the love of my life, my wife Brenda, not only held our family together while this book was being written; she read and edited this book multiple times. First Trust's senior economist, Bob Stein, and chief investment strategist, Bob Carey, can find their ideas and words throughout the book. Strider Elass and Andrew Hull edited, created graphics, and provided essential support. My assistant, Mary Buchanan, helped in more ways than she will ever know. At John Wiley & Sons, my editor and friend, Pamela van Giessen, had the vision for this book, while Emilie Herman, Kate Wood, Stacey Fischkelta, and many others I never had the privledge of getting to know did the heavy lifting to keep it on schedule.

My parents, June and Stu Wesbury, raised me to think freely and always told me that I could do anything I set my mind upon. This book is proof of that. Larry Kohls knows how important he is to me, but hardly ever hears it. Finally, Amity Shlaes went above and beyond the call of duty to write the Foreword to this book. I thank her from the bottom of my heart.

About the Author

Brian Wesbury is chief economist at First Trust Advisors LP, a financial services firm based in Wheaton, Illinois, and serves on the board of advisors to First Trust Capital Partners, an affiliated private-equity firm. He is well known as an entertaining and informative commentator on macroeconomic issues. The *Wall Street Journal* ranked Mr. Wesbury the nation's number one U.S. economic forecaster in 2001, and *USA Today* ranked him as one of the nation's top 10 forecasters in 2004.

Mr. Wesbury writes frequently for the editorial page of the *Wall Street Journal* and is the economics editor of *The American Spectator*. Mr. Wesbury is a member of the Academic Advisory Council of the Federal Reserve Bank of Chicago, and he also sits on the board of managers of Three-Sixty Advisory Group, a Pasadena, California–based consulting and private-equity firm. Mr. Wesbury began his career in 1982 at the Harris Bank in Chicago. Former positions include vice president and economist for the Chicago Corporation and senior vice president and chief economist for Griffin, Kubik, Stephens, & Thompson. In 1995 and 1996, he served as chief economist for the Joint Economic Committee of the U.S. Congress.

For half a decade he taught money and banking as an adjunct professor of economics at Wheaton College in Wheaton, Illinois. Mr. Wesbury received an MBA from Northwestern University's Kellogg Graduate School of Management, and a BA in economics from the University of Montana. His first book, *The New Era of Wealth* was published in 1999. He resides in the western suburbs of Chicago with his wife and two children.

Index